ECONOMIC THEORIES OF
EXHAUSTIBLE RESOURCES

Non-renewable resources pose difficult problems for economists and policy makers who have to evaluate conflicting views about the future availability of resources. When considering current and future rates of consumption, they must look at the role of technological change and examine its bearing upon the way in which alternative resources might be developed. Arguing that the contemporary theory of exhaustible resources is excessively pessimistic, the author of this book is concerned to highlight an optimistic alternative. In examining the writings of prominent authors including Adam Smith, Ricardo, J.S. Mill, Marshall, Gray, and Cassell, he reveals the existence of a significant literature, the essentially optimistic tone of which contrasts with the pessimism of later twentieth-century contributions.

Dr Robinson begins by examining natural resource classification and the nature of return in mining, giving particular emphasis to different sources of long-run price changes in mining and their relevance for user cost and for the economic treatment of exhaustible resources. He then traces the development of the economic theory of exhaustible resources from the last quarter of the eighteenth century to the first quarter of the twentieth, documenting the differing views of various authors about the future availability of mineral resources and the extent of user cost involved in their exploitation. He identifies a link between the perceived availability of exhaustible resources and the nature of the economic theory used to explain their exploitation. Dr Robinson concludes that, since the most important contributions to theory on this subject occur during times of particular concern about the adequacy of natural resources, they are therefore characterized by an undue level of pessimism.

The author

T.J.C. Robinson is Principal Lecturer in Economics at the School of Management, Queensland University of Technology, Brisbane.

Economic Theories of Exhaustible Resources

T. J. C. Robinson

ROUTLEDGE
London and New York

First published 1989 by Routledge
11 New Fetter Lane, London EC4P 4EE
29 West 35th Street, New York, NY 10001

© 1989 T.J.C. Robinson

Printed and bound in Great Britain by
Biddles Ltd, Guildford and King's Lynn

British Library Cataloguing in Publication Data

Robinson, T.J.C. (Timothy John Caldecott, *1945*–
    Economic theories of exhaustible resources.
    1. Natural resources. Exhaustibility. Economic
    aspects
    I. Title
    333.7

    ISBN 0-415-00988-X

Library of Congress Cataloging in Publication Data

Robinson, T.J.C. (Tim J.C.), 1945–
    Economic theories of exhaustible resources / T.J.C. Robinson.
        p.   cm.
    Revision of thesis (doctoral) — University of Queensland, 1987.
    Bibliography: p.
    Includes index.
    ISBN 0-415-00988-X
    1. Nonrenewable natural resources. 2. Economics. I. Title.
HC59.R55   1989
333.7–dc19   88-32447
                                                                        CIP

For Mary

Contents

Foreword

This study reveals that the contemporary economic theory of exhaustible resources relies upon an essentially pessimistic and perhaps unwarranted assumption about the future abundance of mineral resources. In so doing it places the contemporary theory in context by reviewing the literature which preceded it. It is not widely understood that the work of contemporary theorists was preceded by an extensive scholarly literature which stretches back at least to Adam Smith. Although this literature is attributable to some of the most prominent of classical and early neoclassical authors it is testimony to the nature of contemporary economics that this material has remained buried in the works of pioneers whose contributions are often quoted but seldom read. Such is the ignorance of this literature that the contemporary theory of exhaustible resources is widely understood to have been, not the outcome of a process of historical evolution but rather, the result of an act of creation on the part of Harold Hotelling. However, consideration of the literature which preceded Hotelling's famous 1931 article reveals that, when seen in a wider context, the contemporary treatment of exhaustible resources presents a one-sided and highly pessimistic theory which is not representative of these earlier writings.

Hotelling's predecessors displayed varying degrees of optimism about the future availability of mineral resources and in the reviews of their works which are offered later much emphasis is given to this optimism. This emphasis is intentional and is designed to counter the credibility which is accorded the essentially pessimistic contemporary theory. This emphasis may, however, be taken to indicate a great degree of optimism on the part of the author. While admitting to lean towards optimism rather than

Foreword

pessimism in so far as future availability of minerals is concerned, I hasten to add that this optimism does not carry over to all of those resources which constitute our natural and man-made environments. For my own tastes, the rate at which rain forests, wetlands, wilderness and nineteenth century buildings are disappearing is excessive; and, of course, the rate at which these resources are disappearing is not always independent of events which occur in the mineral industries.

In the contemporary literature, the theory of exhaustible resources is, with few exceptions, explained by reference to minerals as representative of this resource type. Although the appropriateness of a classificatory system which, *inter alia*, uses the term 'exhaustible resources' to describe minerals is later addressed in this study, it remains that the contemporary economic theory of exhaustible resources is the economic theory of mining. In assessing this contemporary theory by comparing it with the work of earlier authors it is thus the analysis of the economics of mining presented by these authors which is examined here.

My interest in the subject matter of this study was first aroused during a period when I was investigating mineral and energy economics as a member of the research staff in the Department of Economics at the University of Queensland. Subsequently this subject matter became the focus for my doctoral thesis which was submitted in 1987. Revision of that thesis has resulted in this book.

Some of the ideas in this book have been presented in articles in *Resources Policy*. The articles have not been reproduced but I am grateful to the editor of this journal for permission to use again some of the ideas and some of the phrases which they contain. A significant debt is also due to a number of individuals who have assisted in a variety of ways in the creation of this work. They include Dr A. Brown, Dr S. McL. Cochrane, Lester Deakin, Mr L.A. Duhs, David Dwyer, Mr A. Fitzgibbons, Hazel Imison, Professor H.M. Kolsen, Professor G.D. McColl, Professor C. Robinson, Professor C. Tisdell and Rosemary Tregenza.

T.J.C. Robinson
Queensland University of Technology
Australia

Part I : Some Conceptual and Theoretical Issues

1
Introduction

This work studies the development of the contemporary economic theory of exhaustible resources. It does so by examining the literature produced in the one hundred and fifty year period extending from the last quarter of the eighteenth century to the first quarter of the twentieth. Apart from this time frame, two further limitations have been set to the range of works eligible for review in this study. Firstly, it considers only the work of authors who discussed theoretical mineral economics. Secondly, it is concerned only with contributions to the literature which were either first published in English or translated into English during the period under review. While this work involves reviews of the literature it is, however, not merely a simple account or translation of what the authors reviewed had to say. In tracing developments in the literature it also documents changes in the views which its authors held about the future abundance of mineral resources. This thematic treatment of the contrast between optimistic and pessimistic views of mining also involves comparison, throughout this work, of these developments with the more extensive and better documented development of views about the future abundance of agricultural lands. As the conclusion to this study will show, in spite of wide acceptance of optimistic views about agriculture, the culmination of one hundred and fifty years of analysis of the economics of mining involved the triumph of a generally pessimistic approach.

This chapter serves as both a general introduction to this study and as an introduction to the first of its two parts. Part I of this study is concerned with definitions and ideas, while Part II which is the major part is concerned with assessment of authors who qualify for consideration according to the criteria which have been

3

set down above and which will be further explained later in this chapter.

In 1931 Harold Hotelling's famous article 'The Economics of Exhaustible Resources' was published. This work is considered more than any other to be the seminal work dealing with this topic.[1] In the fourteen years since Robert Solow so effectively brought the thrust of this paper to a contemporary audience in his 1973 Richard T. Ely Lecture there has been a huge growth in the literature dealing with the theoretical treatment of the economics of mining.[2] This literature has been produced in the era of the second modern conservation movement and much of it has been written from a broadly conservationist standpoint; certainly much of it has emphasised the so-called 'cake eating' problem - the problem of the appropriate time-profile of the exploitation of the finite contents of the mine.[3]

This literature is, in this respect, thus essentially similar to Hotelling's earlier treatment. Although Hotelling's paper was written at the end of the period of influence of the first conservation movement at a time when more pressing problems were entering the economic stage, he also saw the problem of the rate at which 'cake' should be eaten as central to a theoretical discussion of mining. That is, he considered the economics of mining to involve the question of the optimal intertemporal allocation of output from the mine (or the nation's mines). A fundamental premiss upon which Hotelling based his analysis of mining was that the 'cake' which might be eaten had not gone stale or mouldy, had not fallen from favour as a result of the superior talents of competing 'bakers', nor had it been found to be carcinogenic or a threat to human happiness in some other way. Hotelling's analysis thus relied on the assumption that the in situ mineral deposit or deposits about which production decisions were made had a capitalised value.[4] However, unlike many of his successors, Hotelling was careful to indicate that the environment in which mineral deposits were assumed to have such a characteristic was one in which resources were exploited in order of accessibility - commencing with the most accessible.[5] As the next two chapters will show, decreasing mineral abundance associated with the need to resort to inferior resources when deposits which are currently being worked are exhausted, confers a capitalised value on these deposits.

At much the same time as Hotelling was formulating his elegant mathematical treatment of the 'cake eating' problem as it related to mining, an Australian author F.R.E. Mauldon, who was responsible for that country's first thoroughgoing mineral industry study, had this to say about conditions in the domestic coal mining industry:

> 'It does not, of course, follow from the fact of great resources that the richest deposits are the first to be worked, though clearly the most remunerative will have prior exploitation. Thus it is true in Australia, as it is in the United States, that the newer mines opening up can be worked under easier rather than harder conditions "imposed by nature." This observation does not overlook the fact that knowledge of the coal resources of the country is not to be gained quickly or purchased without considerable cost. Time and means are needed for both preliminary geological surveys and for the "proving" of coal deposits. This is true of an old coal-producing country like Great Britain, as it is more obviously true of a new country like Australia. Not the costs imposed by nature, however, but the costs imposed by man himself multiply the hazards which, paradoxically enough, make a wide range of coal resources dangerous and embarrassing. The economic problems of coal in no small measure are the difficulties of adjustment to these perils and embarrassments.'[6]

In the Australian coal industry at the time that Hotelling's discussion of the 'cake eating' problem was published, the problem was not one of being unable to 'have cake and eat it too' but rather, a problem of 'having too much cake and eating too little'! Mauldon argued that this problem was the result of a significant increase in supply in an environment of relatively stable demand. As Mauldon notes in the quotation above, in Australia, as in America, there had been a tendency for discovery of richer deposits to follow that of the poorer thus leading, *cet. par.*, to an increase in abundance of the mineral over time. An environment such as this is one which will be shown in the next two chapters to be conducive to low or even zero mineral deposit values.

In the forty years following the publication of Hotelling's and Mauldon's works a generally optimistic attitude to mineral resource availability prevailed and, as is well documented elsewhere, the progeny of Hotelling's seminal work was a long time coming - not until the mid 1970s was the growing concern with the natural resource endowment fertilised in the literature of economics with the seed from Hotelling's article.[7] The outcome of this union was a formalised and well integrated economic treatment of mineral extraction which generally involved the 'cake eating' problem and often took the form of exercises in optimal control theory. Since the mid 1970s there has been a huge growth in this literature; and the volume of material relating to theoretical mineral economics produced after Hotelling's seminal paper but prior to the mid 1970s is miniscule in relation to it. That is, in the period between the influence of the first and second modern conservation movements there were relatively few contributions to the theoretical literature of the economics of mining. Not only were there relatively few contributions made during this period but these contributions also typically gave much less emphasis to the 'cake eating' problem than was given to it in the literature which appeared from the mid 1970s onwards.[8]

The choice of the subject matter for this book was prompted in part by this contrast between the post-Hotelling literature which was published prior to the mid 1970s and that which was published at the height of the influence of the second conservation movement in the late 1970s. The emergence of a generally pessimistic literature at the end of a long period of indifference to the pessimistic seminal work on which it was based posed the question of the nature of the treatment of the subject prior to the emergence of that seminal work.

As well as this largely theoretical contributing factor there was also another influence of a more practical nature which prompted this study. Presenting a theoretical treatment of the mineral industries based on Hotelling's model, Orris Herfindahl in a 1964 paper considered the possible long run progress of output price in contemporary mineral industries.[9] He concluded that the most likely scenario was one in which mineral output prices were roughly equal to extraction costs and, *cet. par.*, remained relatively constant over time. Relating this theoretically explained conclusion to real world events in the mineral industries Herfindahl argued that it shows why practical men in these industries are not particularly concerned to emphasise the finite nature of resource stocks but observe that 'the economic activity of the minerals industries proceeds in much the same way as that of other industries.'[10] Indeed, in spite of the impact of the second conservation movement, many practical men may still be observed to perceive the mineral industries as being economically similar to

other industries. Although the question of whether these men of
the world are correct or not will shortly be seen to be of particular
significance in the context of the review of the literature which
follows, what is important at this stage is that the views of these
practical men are also a factor which prompted this study. For, if
practical men have a picture of the mineral industries which is at
variance with the pessimistic stance of much of the modern
theoretical literature, the question naturally arises as to whether,
in an earlier age, a different picture of the economics of the
mineral industries was presented in the literature.[11]

Finally, this review of the development of the economic analysis
of mining in the approximately one hundred and fifty years prior
to the publication of Hotelling's paper was also prompted by its
seeming, after some initial exploratory research, to be a worthwhile exercise in the history of economic thought.[12]

It was earlier remarked that this study has a leitmotif which
relates to contrasting views about the way in which mineral
abundance changes over time. As has already been indicated, the
contemporary theoretical economic treatment of mining is
generally presented as involving the aforementioned 'cake eating'
problem and thus takes an essentially pessimistic view of mineral
resource availability - emphasising that physical depletion of *in situ*
mineral deposits involves an economic cost. Although this emphasis is apparent in the contemporary literature and although it
was found in Hotelling's seminal work, this study will show that
it has not always been a feature of the literature. Indeed, the first
major theoretical treatment of mining in modern economics is
found in the *Wealth of Nations* and there Adam Smith takes an
essentially optimistic stance in relation to the extent of economic
cost involved in mineral depletion. This optimism was later
confirmed by some of the authors to be reviewed here while others
suggested that a pessimistic stance was warranted. In other cases,
authors suggested that, depending on relevant circumstances,
either of the pessimistic or optimistic scenarios may characterise
the mining process.

The question of whether or not physical depletion involves
economic depletion is one of particular significance for the
assessment of the literature contributed during the period under
review here and a major objective of the remainder of Part I is to
provide a background which will enhance the reader's understanding of this issue. The practice of introducing an economic work
with some background analysis of the terms and concepts em-

7

ployed is one which is perhaps less common today than previously. Regardless of whether or not this perceived change is generally justified, it will become clear that insofar as the subject matter of this work is concerned, there is much to be gained by maintenance of the practice of providing introductory background material. One of the major reasons for the suitability of such an approach is the clear lack of contextual material offered in the contemporary theoretical literature dealing with the subject area under review. Much of this literature eschews the idea of presenting introductory methodological material relating to definitions and ideas; rather, it simply starts where other authors have left off. That is, much of this literature is restricted to refinement, correction or modification of the work of previous authors - and even the work of these previous authors often lacks explicit treatment of underlying assumptions and definitions. The theoretical analysis of mining in the contemporary economic literature is, in many cases, thus bereft of the sort of rigorous background information which befits scientific investigation. Although this literature often has an internal rigour of high order associated with the use of mathematical techniques, it typically proceeds on the basis of a series of crucial but tacit assumptions about aspects such as the type of resource being discussed and the nature of the relevant aspects of physical return involved. The next two chapters which complete Part I are designed to ensure that no such omission occurs in this work.

Chapter 2 deals with the definition of natural resources. At the risk of introducing 'arguments over the exact definition and typology of natural resources [which] provide little more than an intellectual exercise for the tidy mind',[13] this chapter endeavours to put the current system of classification of natural resources into context. In so doing it suggests the use of a classificatory criterion which would not only facilitate a better general appreciation of the natural resource economics literature - including that under review here - but will also help clarify the question of whether mining occurs in an environment of increasing or decreasing mineral resource scarcity.

Chapter 3 deals with the nature of physical return in mining. Its purpose is twofold: firstly, it discusses the nature of historical return with the objective of shedding more light on important aspects of the thematic question of whether mining exists in an environment of increasing or decreasing resource scarcity; secondly, it discusses the particular nature of short run return in mining. In this latter aspect, this chapter discusses some of the difficulties associated with the analysis of short run return. It does so in order to facilitate a better understanding of this aspect of the work of some of the authors who are later reviewed. Although the discussion of historical return in Chapter 3 involves familiar aspects of return, many of these aspects have been contemptuously ignored in the recent literature of the economics of mining. Regardless of the reasons for this situation, it remains that these aspects are of great significance for the theoretical analysis of exhaustible resources. This is particularly true of an investigation such as that undertaken in this work which involves assessment of the formative period in the development of an established body of theory. Whereas, in the contemporary literature it may be excusable for those operating within the strict paradigmatic framework to tacitly maintain the established approach to various underlying aspects of the theory - including those relating to the nature of historical return - it is not excusable to do so in the context of an analysis of the way in which that theory has evolved. For it is precisely the explicit evolution of those aspects now tacitly underlying the contemporary theory which is of signal importance in understanding the way in which the contemporary theory has developed and the significance of the outcome of that development.

As will become evident when the substance of the next two chapters is revealed, these chapters are, like the body of this work, structured in such a way as to minimise the reader's reliance on the particular content of the contemporary body of literature dealing with the theoretical treatment of the economics of exhaustible resources. This approach is purposely undertaken in order that the significance of the contributions of the authors reviewed in Part II of this study can be assessed from a standpoint which is neutral with respect to the contemporary conventional wisdom. This is not to say, however, that the relationship between the work of the authors who are later reviewed here and the body of contemporary theory is an aspect which is ignored in this study. On the contrary, an important feature of the assessment of these authors involves identification of those parts of their work which contributed directly to the development of the contemporary theoretical treatment of the economics of exhaustible resources. The work of these authors will, however, also be assessed in relation to those aspects which have not gained recognition in the contemporary literature.

This having been said, it should be emphasised that this study is, nonetheless, presented within the framework of that basic economic paradigm which is described as involving neoclassical or modern price theory. Thus the significance of the work of the authors who are reviewed in Part II is determined primarily on the basis of criteria set by the general body of contemporary value theory rather than by those suggested by the specific body of applied value theory which deals with the economics of exhaustible resources. In this way, not only can the process of evolution of the contemporary theory of the economics of exhaustible resources be revealed, but the question of the appropriateness of the product of this evolution can also be addressed.

The literature reviewed in Part II of this study involves the work of authors who discussed the economics of mineral extraction in the period from 1776 to 1926. These authors are discussed in chronological order of the publication of their work. The first to be discussed is thus Adam Smith, the last is Gustav Cassel. All but one of the chapters in Part II are concerned with the work of a single author. These chapters look first at the detail of the particular author's contribution, assessing this detail in many of its aspects as it is revealed. At the same time, the dependence of the work being assessed on that of peers and predecessors is also indicated. Each of these chapters then concludes with an overall assessment of the contribution of the author being reviewed.

The one chapter in Part II which does not deal with the work of a single author is Chapter 6 which involves a comparison of the very different treatments of mines which were offered by the first two authors reviewed here - Adam Smith and Ricardo. Although Adam Smith's optimism in relation to mining was later echoed by the American Henry Carey who showed even greater optimism than had Smith, it is noteworthy that Ricardo who was the next of the classical economists to consider mining after Smith, presented a very different and pessimistic prognosis. This conflict of opinion about whether mining is characterised by increasing or decreasing resource scarcity will be seen in Part I to be of particular theoretical significance. It is this theoretical significance, taken with the fact that the introduction of mining into the modern economic literature was associated with conflict between the two most prominent of the classical economists, which has prompted the comparison of Smith and Ricardo in Chapter 6. It is there that an explanation is sought as to why the introduction of mining into the mainstream of modern economics should be characterised by such a difference of opinion as is found between these authors.[14]

Following this diversion, the remainder of Part II continues the chronological overview of the work of authors who succeeded Smith and Ricardo - concluding with the work of Cassel. These chapters contain much novel material and although the contributions to the literature of mineral economics made by the authors under review here have, in some cases, been acknowledged in other works, the assessments which are offered in the following chapters are, as far as the author can ascertain, more comprehensive than any which have been published hitherto.[15] Indeed, insofar as the works of Carey and Cassel in the area of mining are concerned, there appear to be no previous assessments. Not only are there thorough assessments made of the contributions of each of the individual authors who are considered in Part II but, taken together, these chapters also build up a comprehensive picture of the development of the economics of mineral extraction from the last quarter of the eighteenth century to the first quarter of the twentieth.

As well as its significance for the development of economic thought, the review contained in Part II is also of particular contemporary significance - not only from the point of view of its relevance for the verisimilitude of the contemporary theory but also in relation to the bearing which that theory has upon practical matters. Although these practical matters lie outside the scope of this study it is clear that if the actions of persons who control and who regulate the activities of mining firms are based - if only in some cases - on a body of contemporary theory which is founded on a pessimistic premiss, then these actions may well be inappropriate if that premiss is, in turn, inappropriate.

The significance of the work of the authors reviewed in Part II is made clear in the chapters dealing with each of them; and in the Conclusion major consideration is given to the question of the integrity of the theory which had evolved by the end of the review period and to the thematic question of the extent to which optimism or pessimism about the future availability of mineral resources characterised the contributions of the authors reviewed. In relation to this latter aspect, an explanation is sought for the triumph of the pessimistic viewpoint in the twentieth century literature. It is concluded that this has resulted from a tendency for the greatest growth in the neoclassical literature to occur in times of particular concern about the adequacy of the natural resource endowment. In this context, it is interesting that this book is being published at a time when the influence of the second conservation movement appears to be waning. Although it is not possible to say whether history will confirm this trend, it is clear that in questioning the contemporary relevance of a pessimistic theoretical approach by examining the evidence for and against it from authors whose contributions were made in a previous age, the validity of such an approach may be easily justified in a world economic environment such as that which currently prevails where the real prices of most minerals are at historically low levels and where real oil prices are but a fraction of their level in the 1970s.

This introductory chapter would not be complete without some further indication of the limits of the subject matter with which this study deals. This may be achieved by pointing out some of the things which it is not. Firstly, although consideration of the way in which various authors have described and analysed mine surplus is central to this study and although this description and analysis has often involved comparison of mine surplus with farm surplus, this review does not involve a history of the treatment of rent. Secondly, this study is concerned only with the work of economists who specifically discussed theoretical mineral economics and is not concerned with the work of authors who emphasised the general problems of the scantiness of the natural resource endowment. Thus, there is no consideration of the work of prominent authors such as T.R. Malthus and J.B. Clark who, amongst many others, were significant contributors in this area.[16] Lastly, a number of authors writing in the period under review offered statistical or descriptive treatments of mineral activity which were devoid of significant contributions to the theoretical mineral economics literature. These works, the most prominent of which is probably W.S. Jevons's *Coal Question*, are also not a part of the literature which qualifies for review in this study.[17]

Finally, the tagging of Hotelling's paper as the seminal work in the literature dealing with exhaustible resources may, unfortunately, be taken to imply the absence of a significant literature prior to its publication. However, far from being a period lacking in significant works, the one hundred and fifty years prior to the publication of Hotelling's paper will be seen in the chapters which follow, to be a rich source of foundation material. During this period there was formulated a distinctly separate economic treatment of mining which was a fitting precursor to Hotelling's work. It should, however, also be made clear that this formulation did not always involve a process of progressive refinement of ideas which had been presented earlier on. Rather, the development of the economic treatment of mining in this period occurred in chequered fashion - and in no aspect is this more apparent than in relation to the changing views held about the future availability of mineral resources.

Notes

1. H. Hotelling, 'The economics of exhaustible resources', *Journal of Political Economy*, vol. 39 (1931). 'There are only a few fields in economics whose antecedents can be traced to a single, seminal article. One such field is natural resource economics, which is currently experiencing an explosive revival of interest; its origin is widely recognised as Harold Hotelling's 1931 paper...' S. Devarajan and A.C. Fisher, 'Hotelling's "Economics of Exhaustible Resources": fifty years later', *Journal of Economic Literature*, vol. 19 (1981), p. 65.

2. R.M. Solow, 'The economics of resources or the resources of economics', *American Economic Review*, vol. 64 (1974).

3. Anthony Fisher's survey of the literature in his *Resource and environmental economics* (Cambridge University Press, Cambridge, 1981) makes this abundantly clear. See especially chapter 2.

4. 'A pool of oil or vein of iron or deposit of copper in the ground is a capital asset to society and to its owner (in the kind of society in which such things have private owners) much like a printing press or a building or any other reproducible capital asset.' Solow, 'The economics of resources or the resources of economics', p. 2.

5. Hotelling, 'The economics of exhaustible resources', pp. 140-1.

6. F.R.E. Mauldon, *The Economics of Australian Coal* (Melbourne University Press, Melbourne, 1929), pp. 28-9. In a footnote to the first sentence of this quotation Mauldon explains that in New South Wales the relatively poorer deposits in the Newcastle measures were first developed in 1797 while the rich Greta measures were not developed until after 1891.

7. See, for example, Devarajan, 'Hotelling's "Economics of Exhaustible Resources": fifty years later'.

8. This feature is particularly apparent in the extensive literature dealing with the economics of the British coal industry.

9. O.C. Herfindahl, 'Depletion and Economic Theory' in M. Gaffney (ed.), *Extractive Resources and Taxation* (University of Wisconsin Press, Madison, 1967).

10. Ibid., p. 85.

11. This question arises not only because of the possibility that these practical men may be 'the slaves of some defunct economist' but also because differences of opinion between practical men and contemporary academics may, on the other hand, suggest that in some instances the contemporary theory is at fault, the error being found 'not in the superstructure, which has been erected with great care for logical consistency, but in a lack of clearness and of generality in the premises.' J.M. Keynes, *The General Theory of Employment Interest and Money* (Macmillan, London, 1936), p. 383 and p. v.

12. In relation to this aspect, my 1980 *Resources Policy* paper was the outcome of the exploratory research designed to determine, *inter alia*, whether modern economists had produced a sufficient literature prior to Hotelling's seminal work to warrant a full scale study. T.J.C. Robinson, 'Classical foundations of the contemporary economic theory of non-renewable resources', *Resources Policy*, vol. 6, no. 4 (1980).

13. J. McInerney, 'Natural resource economics: the basic analytical principles' in J.A. Butlin (ed.), *Economics and Resources Policy* (Longman, London, 1981), p. 55.

14. Chapter 6 is based on my 1981 *Resources Policy* postscript, the subject matter of which was suggested by an anonymous referee who had earlier reviewed my 1980 *Resources Policy* paper. T.J.C. Robinson, 'Postscript, classical foundations of the contemporary economic theory of non-renewable resources', *Resources Policy*, vol. 7, no. 4 (1981).

15. There are two recent journal articles in which consideration has been given to relevant aspects of the work of some of the authors who are later reviewed here. See P.J. Crabbe, 'The contribution of L.C. Gray to the economic theory of exhaustible natural resources and its roots in the history of economic thought', *Journal of Environmental Economics and Management*, vol. 10 (1983) and B. Fine, 'Landed property and the distinction between royalty and rent', *Land Economics*, vol. 58, no. 3 (1982).

16. Although Malthus's contribution is well known, J.B. Clark's is not. See J.B. Clark, 'The economics of waste and conservation', *Atlantic Monthly*, vol. 106 (1910).

17. W.S. Jevons, *The Coal Question*, 3rd edn (Macmillan, London, 1906). I am indebted to Professor Colin Robinson who has reminded me that although Jevons did not discuss the theory of the mine, his prognosis of diminishing return on the extensive margin in the British coal industry is, nonetheless, a particularly significant example of nineteenth century pessimism.

2

The Classification of Natural Resources

This chapter deals with the classification of natural resources and has two major objectives. The first of these involves the introduction of some rigour into the general classification of natural resources; while the second is directed towards a clear statement of the characteristics of the natural resources with which this work is concerned.

A feature of almost all of the more recent literature dealing with the economics of natural resources is the tacit but perhaps unwarranted assumption contained therein that the reader has a clear idea of the characteristics of the class of natural resources being discussed. This chapter is designed to prevent the necessity for any such assumption in the case of this work. It considers the definition of natural resources from a contemporary viewpoint; that is, it is concerned with a modern classification of natural resources which may be used, in examining the historical period under consideration, to identify and interpret those parts of the literature which are relevant.

This chapter commences with two introductory sections which discuss in turn the historical background to classification and the economics of classificatory systems. These introductory sections are followed by a section dealing with the system of classification of natural resources which is current. This section lays the foundation for the discussion of an alternative system of classification which, it is argued, may have certain advantages over the current system. Finally, the characteristics of the resources with which this work is concerned are identified.

The Historical Background

The search for scientific classificatory criteria has been a long and arduous one which was characterized initially (especially in the physical sciences) by a desire for rigour above all. More recently, in the physical sciences, a search for practicality which has always pervaded the economic literature has become more evident.

There is an enormous literature dealing, *inter alia*, with the construction of classificatory systems. While it is not an objective of this chapter to provide a critique of this literature, it does consider briefly the contributions made by some prominent economists.

In so far as logical or rigorous criteria are concerned, classificatory systems may be described as involving the application of preconceived ideas or hypotheses in such a way as to permit the taking of 'a set of people or collectives ... and to partition them into a number of *exhaustive* and *mutually exclusive* subsets.'[1] W.S. Jevons clearly indicated the nature and objectives of classification in the definition which he offered in his *Principles of Science*:

> 'By classification of any series of objects, is meant the actual or ideal arrangements together of those which are like and the separation of those which are unlike, the purpose of this arrangement being, primarily to disclose the correlations or laws of union of properties and circumstances, and, secondarily, to facilitate the operations of the mind in clearly conceiving and retaining in the memory the characters of the objects in question.'[2]

In the recent literature of both the physical sciences and the social sciences increasing emphasis has been placed on the practicality or productivity of systems of classification. It is not surprising that in the field of economics, this tradition of practicality is as old as modern economics itself. Witness Malthus's persuasive argument in his *Definitions in Political Economy*:

> '[I]t has been suggested, that a new and more perfect [economic] nomenclature should be introduced. But though the inconveniences of a new nomenclature are much more than counter-balanced by its obvious utility in such sciences

as chemistry, botany, and some others, where a great variety of objects, not in general use, must be arranged and described so as best to enable us to remember their characteristic distinctions; yet in such sciences as morals, politics, and political economy, where the terms are comparatively few, and of constant application in the daily concerns of life, it is impossible to suppose that an entirely new nomenclature would be submitted to; and if it were, it would not render the same service to these sciences, in promoting their advancement, as the nomenclature of Linnaeus, and Cuvier, to the sciences to which they were respectively applied.

Under these circumstances, it may be desirable to consider what seems to be the most obvious and natural rules for our guidance in defining and applying the terms used in the science of political economy. The object to be kept in view should evidently be such a definition and application of these terms, as will enable us most clearly and conveniently to explain the nature and causes of the wealth of nations...'[3]

In his *Principles*, Marshall argues in similar vein.[4] So does L.M. Fraser in his work devoted to language and classification in economics:

'The economist must disentangle those elements in the economic world which can be explained in terms of theoretical principles, and must mark these off from the irregular and (from his point of view) accidental variations that characterise particular instances. His search is for *significant generalisations*; for those classifications of his subject-matter by means of which he can explain and illuminate what is going on.'[5]

Earlier, Fraser argues for maintenance of the tradition that economic language be integrated with everyday language:

'The verbal difficulty [associated with the inaccuracy of economists' linguistic equipment] will not be solved, however, by elaborating a scientific system of insignificant terms. We may sympathise with Mr. Robertson when he demands for economists the right, accorded to researches in other fields of study, to 'speak to one another in their own jargon'. But we cannot afford to allow our language to cut us completely off from ordinary life. For economics, unlike physics or biology, is a study of human behaviour'.[6]

It would seem that this latter cause - the everyday intelligibility of economic language - may have been all but lost in recent times and this aspect is considered further at a later stage in this chapter. This chapter attempts to continue the tradition of usefulness or practicality of economic language and classification, with the proviso that a pragmatic approach such as this must fulfill the objectives of exhaustiveness and mutual exclusivity.

Finally, the need for continual revision of language and of classification such as is occurring here is well summed up by Fraser:

'If economists as a whole were to adopt a corpus of technical terms, each one with an unalterable meaning and content, there would be a real danger of their being left behind by the march of events. A static terminology is not well suited to the study of dynamic phenomena.[7]'

The history of classification in economics is the history of attempts to make systems of classification more productive (or of attempts to help them retain their productivity). Indeed, some of the more recent literature dealing with language and systems of classification is couched specifically in the language of utilitarian economics rather than in more general, everyday language. This literature, which is considered in the next section, is part of the growing literature which purveys a so-called 'economic approach' to human behaviour.

The Economics of Classificatory Systems

'Speech has been called a socio-economic device for saving effort in the attainment of objectives.'[8]   In the language of economics, a language may be described as a factor of production in the sense that it is an 'original resource' or an 'original productive element' which may exist in various forms or qualities each of which may, in combination with other factors, be more or less productive than others.[9] In the same way, a system of classification may also be described as a factor of production.

Once classificatory systems are thought of as factors of production, it follows that they may be considered to have high or low degrees of productivity. This idea is presumably as old as language itself and although its treatment in the specific context of utilitarian economics is quite recent, it has been argued above that it has been recognized by economists since the birth of modern economics. In the context of this chapter, one of the questions which arises from this view of classificatory systems is whether the existing system of economic classification of natural resources can be made more productive and, if so, whether the cost involved is justified. In this regard, the question arises as to whether the modern utilitarian approach to human behaviour (the 'economic approach') will shed light on the matter.

It is a basic tenet of the economic approach to human behaviour that the best economists are economic agents themselves. In other words, since human behaviour is the behaviour of rational, optimising beings there is no normative or prescriptive role for economists - except that of arguing the foregoing case.[10] And, in this context it is a little surprising that advocates of this approach have not argued that their own conclusions (concerning the social phenomena of crime and punishment, extra-marital affairs, religious belief etc.) are so self evident as to be superfluous.[11] If an 'economic approach' to the question of the classification of natural resources were taken, the only conclusion which might reasonably be drawn is that the current classificatory system which has evolved over time is the optimum system. Milton Friedman, in one of his most recent volumes, argues that language with all its shortcomings is an outstanding product of the invisible hand. Friedman goes on to argue, however, that intervention and rule making in the search for more productive language and systems of classification is warranted in the physical and social sciences.[12] Whereas intervention is not required in the realm of everyday language, in the field of science in which Friedman is prominent, intervention is justified. It seems then, that even from the most liberal viewpoint, attempts to improve the productivity of classificatory systems are justified.

Whether there is a case for designing a better or different system of classification of natural resources than the one which is current will depend, *inter alia*, on the suitability of the current system. In the next section the current system of classification is reviewed.

The Current System of Classification of Natural Resources

Is there indeed a system of classification of natural resources which is generally accepted today? Despite the existence of a large number of classificatory terms which are currently used in the literature of economics (including indestructible, exhaustible, depletable, extractive, reproducible, renewable and replenishable) and despite a lack of concurrence as to the type of resource to which each term refers (for example, a prominent economist has recently declared mineral oil to be a renewable resource),[13] there appears to be a tacitly accepted classification of natural resources which involves three broad classes. These are: i) The *indestructible* class, ii) the *renewable* class, and iii) the *exhaustible* class. This system of classification had been developed by Marshall's time - if not in Ricardo's - although the debate as to which resources fit into each class has not finally been resolved.[14]

Indestructible resources may be defined as: 'resource stocks which, although they are not augmentable, are not permanently depleted as a result of their productive use.' It is Ricardo who is attributed with the origin of the indestructible class, and the argument as to whether agricultural land is, indeed, indestructible has been going on since his time. Despite general agreement that the productive powers of the soil need to be replenished periodically and that land's location (that is, the notion of territory) is its only really indestructible feature, it continues to be thought of as having the characteristics indicated by the above definition.[15] Other resources which are tacitly taken to be indestructible, correctly or otherwise, include the oceans and the atmosphere.

Renewable resources may be defined as: 'resource stocks which, being augmentable, may be reversibly depleted in the process of their productive use.' Renewable resources include fauna, flora and marine life in their natural states as well as domesticated animals and crops. It appears that in the nineteenth century literature, the indispensable role that crops and farm animals play in the productive process was largely ignored, having been swamped by the debate about the role of land as a factor of production and as a source of rent. Although other renewable resources such as forests and fisheries are discussed in this literature the former have been construed as exhaustible (akin to minerals) and the latter as indestructible (akin to land).[16] It was not until the present century that terms such as renewable and replenishable were applied to these resources and so gained general usage.

Exhaustible resources are unlike indestructible or renewable resources in that their productive use must involve permanent depletion of the extant stock. They may be defined as: 'resource stocks which are not augmentable and which are always irreversibly depleted in the process of their productive use.' Naturally, the most important category of exhaustible resources is minerals and while nineteenth century economists spoke of minerals as being exhaustible, their investigations were more likely to have been described as the economics of mines rather than the economics of exhaustible resources. Only since the publication of Lewis Gray's paper 'Rent Under the Assumption of Exhaustibility' has the term exhaustible gained parlance.[17] More recently, the term non-renewable has often been used interchangeably with exhaustible.

Having described the current system of natural resource classification, the question of whether it is an adequate (sufficiently productive) system can now be addressed. To assist in answering this question it is first necessary to investigate the underlying criterion which forms the basis for the traditional classificatory schema outlined above.

The traditional system of classification is essentially a classification based on a single criterion; namely, the degree of exhaustibility of a resource in productive use. Now, the significance of exhaustibility is that it implies that present use precludes the potential for future use; that is, that present and future uses are antagonistic. Clearly, exhaustibility can be considered to exist in degree and there may thus be greater or lesser degrees of antagonism between present and future uses. The degree of exhaustibility of a resource may be indicated by what we shall call its *net depletion rate*.

The net depletion rate of a specific resource stock is here defined as the outcome of the relationship between the rate of physical depletion which is associated with productive use (gross depletion) and the rate at which physical rejuvenation of the resource occurs. That is, for any given rate of gross depletion of a resource, the net depletion rate or degree of exhaustibility will be determined by the extent to which rejuvenation occurs; and the rate at which rejuvenation occurs will depend on the rate at which any natural or unaided rejuvenation occurs and the extent to which this natural or unaided rate is accelerated by man.

Naturally occurring or unaided rejuvenation rates, while having economic significance for nomadic communities, often have little relevance in the determination of the degree of exhaustibility of resources which are being exploited by sedentary communities. For example, although agricultural land displays low natural rejuvenation rates, it generally has a low net depletion rate (is considered indestructible) since in many cases, especially those associated with private ownership, the acceleration of natural rejuvenation rates by fertilising and tilling is worthwhile and actual rejuvenation rates are high. Thus indestructible resources typically have zero or very low net depletion rates in productive use.

In the case of renewable resources, there are some resources for which the incurring of costs for accelerated rejuvenation is not worthwhile - often because the resource is publicly owned and the benefit associated with accelerating rejuvenation cannot be appropriated. In this regard, resources such as deep sea fisheries and game come to mind. In other cases of renewable resources (especially where private ownership occurs) it is accelerated rejuvenation rates which are relevant. In many of these cases augmentation of the resource stock may occur. That is, accelerated rejuvenation may exceed gross depletion to give a negative net depletion rate. Examples of this latter case of renewable resources include domesticated farm animals and crops. From this discussion of renewable resources it can be seen that they may display positive, zero or negative net depletion rates in productive use.

The most important group of exhaustible resources is minerals and, for most minerals, natural rejuvenation rates are so low that they can be taken to be zero. In this respect, minerals are different from renewable or indestructible resources in that the productive use of minerals will involve gross and net depletion rates which are identical and which are always positive. That is, exhaustible resources are resources which have only positive net depletion rates in productive use.

For each class of natural resources identified in the traditional schema there will be a net depletion rate associated with productive use and this net depletion rate will depend, *cet. par.*, on the relationship between the costs of waiting for rejuvenation to occur naturally, if at all, and the costs of bringing rejuvenation forward in time.[18]

In the light of the foregoing discussion, what can be said about the practicality (productivity) of the traditional system of classification? It can be considered in relation to the following aspects:

a) the extent to which this system of classification facilitates the rigorous segregation of resources in a mutually exclusive way;

b) the degree to which the system is an economic, as opposed to a technical system;

c) the extent to which the relationship between the economic meaning of the terms involved and their everyday meaning assists or detracts from their usefulness.

In relation to the first aspect, it can be seen that the class to which a resource belongs is to some extent arbitrary and dependent upon historical accident. For example, why should the fertility of the soil be considered indestructible while other resources which are also managed in such a way as to involve zero net depletion are considered as renewable? Examples of the latter include some forests and freshwater fisheries. On the other hand, we have seen that minerals have sometimes been classified as renewable rather than exhaustible since the effect of their depletion is to call forth 'rejuvenation' in the form of new discoveries. The arbitrary fashion in which resources have been classified brings with it a reluctance, on the part of economists, to alter the classification of a specific resource when changes in its characteristics occur over historical time. For example, in the 1960s, it was non-economists who pointed out to economists that resources such as clean air and water should no longer be classed as indestructible but should, by virtue of their showing a positive net depletion rate, be classed as renewable.

The second aspect to be considered in relation to the productivity of the traditional system of classification is whether the system is essentially technical or economic. The traditional classificatory system indicates whether productive use of the resource is likely to result in no change in the physical stock, in a change of the physical stock which may be positive or negative or finally, a change which is always negative. It does not, however, indicate the economic significance of these changes. This aspect can be well illustrated by considering the case of exhaustible resources. Later in this work it will be shown that some authors have suggested that, in spite of their physical depletion, certain minerals may be becoming more rather than less abundant over time. If changes in technology or the development of externalities associated with economic growth are responsible for altering the rank ordering of mineral deposits (according to production cost) over time, then mineral deposits which once were superior may become marginal as they are displaced by newly discovered or previously marginal deposits which, as a result of change, have become the superior deposits. In such cases, the mineral in question is, in many important ways, more akin to a renewable or indestructible resource than it is to an exhaustible resource. This possibility has been given little emphasis in the contemporary theoretical literature - presumably because deductive modes of thought have so excluded induction that it has become traditional to consider that since all minerals display positive net depletion rates in productive use they belong to the exhaustible class and are best analysed by the largely pessimistic body of theory which has been devoted to this class.[19] However, the fact that the productive use of minerals always reduces the absolute physical stock is not necessarily indicative of the antagonism between present and future production which is implied by the label 'exhaustible'. Physical depletion is not synonymous with economic depletion.

The preceding discussion of the first two aspects of the suitability of the traditional system of classification provides a convenient basis for brief mention of the third aspect - its suitability in relation to the economic connotation which the terms it uses may have as compared to their everyday connotation. Obviously there are great advantages for both those in the economics profession and for others, in a system of classification which indicates to non-economists the type of resource to which reference is made in economic writing. However, if it is true, as suggested above, that economists themselves display inconsistencies in assigning resources to each of the traditional classes, then it is so much more likely that non-economists will incorrectly infer from the everyday meaning of the classificatory terms employed, that certain resources have a familiar set of characteristics which go with that everyday meaning. Thus, from an everyday point of view, all resources may be thought of as exhaustible - even those which economists describe as renewable or indestructible. This aspect of classification is further discussed at a later stage in this chapter when the possibility of a modified traditional system of classification is discussed.

In summary, the traditional system of classification is the result of historical evolution; it fails to classify resources rigorously in a mutually exclusive way; it uses a combination of technical and economic criteria; and finally, it uses everyday terms which lead to confusion amongst economists and non-economists alike.

Clearly, there are limitations to the productivity of the current system. But this is not to say that it is not the best system of classification. This is especially so if the costs of substituting an alternative system are considered. Nonetheless, it appears that a case has been made for consideration of an alternative or, at least, an additional system of classification.

An Alternative System

The traditional system of classification which has developed since Ricardo's time and which tacitly uses net depletion in productive use as its classificatory criterion, is essentially a classification based upon the natural resource costs involved in putting these resources to productive use. In this system, rather than using cost itself, its proxy the degree of physical depletion in productive use is employed. Thus this system indicates, for example, that on the one hand, land's location *may* be productively employed without cost (no net depletion) while on the other, minerals can *only* be employed if a cost is incurred (net depletion is always positive). The previously discussed shortcomings of this system occur, in the main, precisely because a technical criterion (physical depletion) is construed as being economic. Much of the blame for this confusion can be attributed to the tradition of maintaining a link between economic and everyday language; for there are no everyday terms which may be used to describe natural resources on the basis of *potential costs incurred* in productive use, in the way that the terms used in the traditional classification describe natural resources on the basis of the *potential for physical depletion* in productive use. There is, however, an existing economic term which may be used, in association with qualifying terms, to indicate the extent to which use of a resource involves cost rather than physical depletion. This term is *user cost*.

In the literature, user cost is described as a variable cost which can be attributed to the wear and tear of machinery which results from current output. It is reckoned net of any maintenance costs which are obviated by the machine's use (for example, the cost of keeping the working parts of an unused machine free from corrosion).[20] This definition of user cost is directly attributable to Keynes's formulation in his appendix to Chapter 6 in the *General*

Theory.[21] Now, the concept of user cost may be as fruitfully applied to assets such as natural resources as it is to machinery or other fixed capital.[22] In the case of natural resources, user cost will relate to wear and tear (depletion) of the resource associated with current production and it will be reckoned net of any costs obviated by use of the resource (for example, keeping fallow ground free from weeds) but inclusive of any improvement (negative cost) associated with non-use of the resource (for example, rejuvenation in the form of organic growth).

Whereas depreciation in the value of an asset may result from wear and tear associated with current output, from natural deterioration, or from obsolescence, *user cost* involves only the first of these factors. User cost is the cost incurred when production in future time periods is precluded by production in the current time period. That is, it is 'the present value of the future profit foregone by a decision to produce a unit of output today'.[23]

The relationship between obsolescence, natural deterioration or improvement and user cost is a complex one and it is not intended to treat it in a definitive way in this chapter.[24] Some useful generalisations can, however, be made. Firstly, *cet. par.*, the more important are the factors of obsolescence or natural deterioration in determining the productive life of a resource, the less important will be the role of user cost. If obsolescence or natural deterioration are occurring at a rapid rate then, *cet. par.*, future profit foregone by a decision to produce today (user cost) will be less that if obsolescence or deterioration are occurring at low rates. If the limit to the productive life of a resource is determined by obsolescence or by complete deterioration which occurs instantaneously, the user cost for the period until the instant when obsolescence or complete deterioration occurs will be zero. For example, the user cost of extraction from a mineral deposit which will become obsolete on a certain day (following, say, the opening of a new, lower cost mine) will be zero for the period up to that day - although user cost may be positive for periods shorter than this.

Secondly, *cet. par.*, the more important is the factor of improvement (as a result, say, of organic growth) in relation to obsolescence (if it is important at all), the more important will be user cost. That is, the user cost of growing resources will be relatively high. The prohibition of the taking of the young and the females of certain species of publicly owned resources reflects this fact. For example, fisheries are often controlled by the enforcement of limits to the size and sex of fish and crustaceans which may be taken.

Finally, two special cases may be noted. Firstly, in the case of extant land's location, which is not depleted by its productive use, there will be no user cost; and even this seemingly incontrovertible proposition may not be true. Bikini Atoll is testimony to the fact that the economic use of land (terra firma) may involve depletion in the territorial sense - another example of the pitfalls of the application of deductive rather than inductive modes of thought. The second special case relates to organic resources which have a life-cycle and which may be depleted to such an extent that regeneration is no longer possible. That is, extinction occurs. In this case, if future availability of the resource has great present value, the user cost of the depletion which coincides with extinction may be very high.[25]

In his appendix to Chapter 6 of the *General Theory*, Keynes argued that user cost had, by and large, been ignored in previous discussions of marginal cost - most authors proceeding under the assumption that it was a negligible part of this cost.[26] While this may be true of discussions of cost in agriculture and in manufacturing, it is not true of many of the discussions of mining - although the specific term 'user cost' was not employed. As later chapters will show, the antagonism between present and future mineral production which user cost measures was clearly identified by many authors who contributed to the modern treatment of the economics of mines before and after the turn of the century.

The preceding discussion of user cost reveals that accurate conclusions cannot necessarily be drawn about the economic characteristics of natural resources on the basis of a largely technical criterion such as the physical depletion rate in productive use. It has been shown that the user cost of 'indestructible' resources may be high while that of 'exhaustible' resources may be low. Classification of resources on the basis of user cost incurred in productive use would, at least from the economist's point of view, much better indicate the economic characteristics of resources which are the subject of economic analysis. Such a classificatory system will rely, of course, on a prior (inductive) knowledge of the extent of user cost involved in the economic use of any particular resource at any particular time. For example, inductive investigation of predatory use of agricultural or grazing land may indicate that it belongs to a high user cost class of natural resources and may thus be subject to deductive economic analysis based on the corpus of theory relating to high user cost resources. A non-predatory use of land may, on the other hand, involve the inclusion of this land in a low or zero user cost class which would indicate a deductive economic analysis based on the theoretical treatment of low or zero user cost resources. Likewise, the economic analysis of mines may be the subject of different deductive analytical approaches depending on whether the mineral in question is determined to be a high, low or zero user cost resource. In this respect, a system of classification based on user cost is no different from the traditional system. By induction, resources are placed in the appropriate class in the traditional system (for example, mines in the exhaustible class) and are then subject to deductive economic analysis based on the corpus of theory devoted to that class (for example, 'the economic theory of exhaustible resources').

Although, from the economist's point of view, natural resources might be better classified on the basis of user cost, the question arises as to whether such a classification would further erode the link between economic and everyday language.

The term *user cost* means, and can be expected to mean little to the non-economist. But this is true of most specialised economic terms. If a more rigorous system of classification based on user cost were adopted, this would certainly bring the economics of natural resources into line with many other areas of applied economics.[27] At the same time, it would prevent non-economists (and economists) from drawing inappropriate conclusions on the basis of the everyday meaning of the terms employed in the traditional classificatory system. This having been said, it should be pointed out that the classificatory terms suggested by a system based on user cost and those employed in the traditional classification are not mutually exclusive. A solution to the problem of maintaining a link between everyday language and economic language may thus be sought in a combination of the rigour of a classificatory system involving user cost with the generality of the traditional system which uses everyday terms. Thus, for example, high, low or zero user cost exhaustible resources could be identified as could high, low or zero user cost renewable resources etc.[28] Such a combination of terms allows a continuity of language over time which effectively reduces the cost of changes associated with attempts to introduce greater rigour into classification.

There has recently been an enormous growth in the specialist literature dealing with the economics of natural resources. In advancing this literature, most authors have tacitly accepted a system of classification which sacrifices rigour in order to satisfy a long standing tradition of facilitating the everyday understanding of economic terms. Although the requirements of this tradition have been relaxed in other areas of economics, it seems that in the area of classification of natural resources the tradition may be maintained if the established system of classification is made more productive by qualifying the terms used therein with reference to the degree of user cost involved.

Earlier in this chapter it was argued that one of its purposes was to assist in identification of the characteristics of the class of resources to which this work refers. This aspect is further considered in the conclusion below.

Conclusion

This study is concerned with the development of a branch of economic theory which is today most commonly called 'the economic theory of exhaustible resources'. It has been argued above that, for a number of reasons, the term 'exhaustible resources' is an imperfect one. On the one hand, its everyday connotation means that it may be construed as dealing with both resources which always have positive net depletion rates in productive use (minerals) and those which may have zero or negative net depletion rates (land and biological resources). On the other hand, in the specialised economic literature this term has come to have a highly restricted connotation since much of the corpus of deductive economic theory which has evolved under the title of 'the economics of exhaustible resources' has relied on the assumption that since exploitation of exhaustible resources always involves positive net depletion rates it necessarily involves user cost. While there are many examples of this approach which might be quoted, the recent review of the theory by Peterson and Fisher amply illustrates the point. Although the authors point out that user cost associated with exhaustible resources may have relatively high or low values and that user cost may rise or fall over time, their review commences with the tacit assumption that exploitation of exhaustible resources does involve user cost; that is, that resource stocks which are being exploited have a capitalised value which, *cet. par.*, falls as extraction proceeds.[29] This initial assumption has - with few notable exceptions - been an integral part of the economic theory of exhaustible resources since the publication of Hotelling's seminal article. It should also be noted that the great bulk of this twentieth century literature dealing with the economics of exhaustible resources has been produced during periods of socially perceived resource scarcity when real output prices and resource stock values have been rising significantly. This aspect is further discussed in the conclusion to this work.

Although the bulk of the twentieth century mineral economics literature emphasises the importance of user cost, later chapters will show that some early economists' considerations of resources of the type which always involve positive net depletion rates in productive use indicate that the user cost of exploitation of these resources may be relatively low or even zero. In spite of the inevitability of physical depletion and in spite of arguments to the contrary, these authors argued that physical depletion of a finite resource stock might not involve economic depletion.

For the reasons indicated above, it is clear that to describe the class of resources with which this review is concerned as 'exhaustible' is to invite the inference that this study is concerned with high user cost resources. Such an inference would, however, be inappropriate and it should be emphasised that no particular degree of user cost is here implied by use of the term 'exhaustible resources'. Indeed, one of the major questions which this study seeks to answer is that of the extent to which the authors reviewed here believed user cost to be relevant to exhaustible resource extraction.

Notes

1. P.F. Lazarsfeld, A.K. Pasanella and M. Rosenberg (eds), *Continuities in the Language of Social Research* (Free Press, New York, 1972), p. 9, emphasis added.

2. W.S. Jevons, *The Principles of Science*, 2nd edn (Macmillan, London, 1877), p. 677. Jevons explains that this is a modified version of a definition first given by Professor Thomas Huxley.

3. T.R. Malthus, *Definitions in Political Economy* (Kelley, New York, 1963), pp. 3-4.

4. See A. Marshall, *Principles of Economics*, 8th edn (Macmillan, London, 1920, 1949, resetting), bk 2, ch. 1.

5. L.M. Fraser, *Economic Thought and Language* (A and C Black, London, 1947), pp. 14-15, original emphasis.

6. Ibid., p. vii.

7. Ibid., pp. vii-viii.

8. M. Critchley, *The Divine Banquet of the Brain and Other Essays* (Raven Press, New York, 1979), p. 45.

9. See Fraser, *Economic Thought*, ch. 12 especially pp. 198-9 and pp. 210-11.

10. See G.S. Becker, *The Economic Approach to Human Behaviour* (University of Chicago Press, Chicago, 1976).

11. 'Liberals are criticizing or constructing economic policies on assumptions which make any policy at all absurdly superfluous.' T.W. Hutchison, *The Significance and Basic Postulates of Economic Theory* (Kelley, New York, 1965), p. 183. First published in 1936.

12. M. and R. Friedman, *Free to Choose* (Harcourt Brace Jovanovich, New York, 1980), pp. 25-6.

13. 'To speak of discoveries, of course, refutes the idea of oil as a non-renewable resource. The economic asset oil reserves are (sic) certainly renewable and replaceable by the economic process of finding and improved recovery.' M.A. Adelman, 'The world oil cartel: scarcity, economics, and politics', *Quarterly Review of Economics and Business*, Summer Issue (1976). Adelman's statement may be compared with the following from R.S. Pindyck: 'Given the economic incentives, reserves can be maintained or increased through further exploration - even though the physical returns in exploration decrease as "depletion" ensues. It therefore makes more sense to think of resources like oil and uranium as being "nonrenewable", rather than "exhaustible".' R.S. Pindyck, 'The optimal exploration and production of nonrenewable resources', *Journal of Political Economy*, vol. 86, no. 51 (1978), pp. 842-3.

14. This system of classification has evolved through a process of common usage. It has done so in spite of attempts by notable authors such as Lewis Gray and Ciriacy-Wantrup to promote more rigorous systems which involve greater complexity. See L.C. Gray, 'The economic possibilities of conservation', *Quarterly Journal of Economics*, vol. 27 (1913), pp. 499-500 and S.V. Ciriacy-Wantrup, *Resource Conservation Economics and Policies* (University of California Press, Berkeley, 1952), ch. 3.

15. The case for considering the soil to be destructible has been well put by Lewis Gray. See chapter 12 below. It has also been long recognized that land is to some extent augmentable.

16. See D. Ricardo, *The Principles of Political Economy and Taxation* (Dent, London, 1911), and Marshall, *Principles*, p. 138 respectively.

17. The term 'exhaustible' was also used in the title of Hotelling's celebrated work. H. Hotelling, 'The economics of exhaustible resources', *Journal of Political Economy*, vol. 39 (1931).

18. For most minerals the net depletion rate is affected by recycling (which in the case of precious metals and gemstones may be quite high). However, recycling may be a feature in the reduction of net depletion rates for almost all natural resources including, contrary to popular belief, fossil fuels. Costs and revenues relevant to depletion of all natural resources will thus depend, *cet. par.*, upon any recycling that occurs. With respect to recycling of fossil fuels, it appears to have become a truism that because of their extreme change in physical form following productive use, they are unable to be recycled and are thus distinctly different from other exhaustible resources. This stems from the consideration of recycling as a technical rather than economic phenomenon. Clearly, if fossil fuels are used to produce physical output and if the recycling of a unit of output requires a smaller energy input than is required to produce a new unit of output of equivalent quality, then this recycling has resulted in a reduction in the *in situ* energy input required per unit output. This occurs in the same way that recycling of metals or timber reduces the *in situ* non-energy input required per unit output. The conventional view that fossil fuels are not recyclable can be found in D.W. Pearce, *Environmental Economics* (Longman, London, 1976), p. 145; R.M. Peterson and A.C. Fisher, 'The exploitation of extractive resources a survey',

Economic Journal, vol. 87 (1977), p. 692, and M.C. Weinstein and R.J. Zeckhauser, 'Use patterns for depletable and recyclable resources' in *Symposium on the Economics of Exhaustible Resources (Review of Economic Studies, 1974)*, p. 67. See also Fraser, *Economic Thought*, pp. 255-60.

19. Anthony Fisher makes it clear in his review of the contemporary theory of exhaustible resources that this theory is quite adequate to the task of assimilating mineral resource augmenting change. It remains, however, that the theory has its foundation in the pessimistic idea that physical depletion involves economic depletion: 'How is an exhaustible resource different from an ordinary good or resource? Simply in that it is limited in quantity and is not producible. But this means that extraction and consumption of a unit today involves an *opportunity cost*: the value that might have been obtained at some future date.' A.C. Fisher, *Resources and environmental economics* (Cambridge University Press, Cambridge, 1981), pp. 12-13, original emphasis.

20. See P.J.D. Wiles, *Price Cost and Output* (Blackwell, Oxford, 1956), p. 9.

21. J.M. Keynes, *The General Theory of Employment Interest and Money* (Macmillan, London, 1936).

22. For a comprehensive treatment of the role of user cost in mineral exploitation see: A.T. Scott, 'The theory of the mine under conditions of certainty' in M. Gaffney (ed.), *Extractive Resources and Taxation* (University of Wisconsin Press, Madison, 1967). A less formal discussion of the role of user cost may be found in P. Davidson, 'The Economics of Natural Resources', *Challenge*, vol. 22 (1979).

23. Scott, 'The theory of the mine', p. 34.

24. Peterson and Fisher offer a definitive treatment of the last two of these factors in their survey. Peterson, 'The exploitation of extractive resources a survey'.

25. This is Ciriacy-Wantrup's case of resources having a 'critical zone'. S.V. Ciriacy-Wantrup, *Resource Conservation*, ch. 3.

26. Keynes, *The General Theory*, p. 72. Keynes goes on: 'In the case of raw materials the necessity of allowing for user cost is obvious; - if a ton of copper is used up to-day it cannot be used to-morrow, and the value which the copper would have for the purposes of to-morrow must clearly be reckoned as a part of the marginal cost.' Ibid., p. 73.

27. It is not without a knowledge of objections to such an approach that this suggestion is made. To reduce natural resources to abstractions involves objections similar to those made by Cropsey with respect to commodities: '[In welfare economics, commodities] are obscured by their reduction to the plane of undifferentiated utility: not as shoes and apples but as the sources of general "utility" are they made the subjects of theory.' J. Cropsey, 'What is Welfare Economics?', *Ethics*, vol. 65, no. 2 (1955), p. 117.

28. There are precedents for such an approach in the literature. John Ise in his pessimistic paper published in 1925 chose to describe the resources which were the subject of this paper as 'quickly exhaustible', and Hotelling in his 1931 paper dealing with exhaustible resources distinguishes 'semi-replaceable assets' from 'absolutely irreplaceable assets'. J. Ise, 'The theory of value as applied to natural resources', *American Economic Review*, vol. 15 (1925) and Hotelling, 'The economics of exhaustible resources'.

29. Peterson, 'The exploitation of extractive resources a survey', part III. See also the quotation to this effect from Fisher in note 22 above.

3

The Nature of Return in Mining

The nature of mining is such that it may be distinguished from other natural resource based industries by virtue of the economically irreversible physical depletion of the resource stock (the *in situ* mineral) which takes place as production occurs. It is as a result of this distinguishing feature that a separate branch of applied economic theory dealing with mineral extraction (with the economics of 'exhaustible' resources) has evolved.

Although this specialised body of theory has many facets, one of its major aspects is that which deals with the optimal rate of extraction from the finite *in situ* mineral deposit. Whereas the treatment of mining by the classical economists has been described as constituting an appendix to the theory of agricultural rent,[1] the neoclassical literature has developed in such a way as to form a separate branch of theory in its own right. While this literature traverses many areas of theoretical economics, its major debt is to the neoclassical capital theory which was developed around the turn of the century. This feature of the literature is demonstrated by its preoccupation with the question of the optimum intertemporal allocation of output from the individual mine. Whereas agriculture and manufacturing are generally considered to involve little or no antagonism between present and future production, in the case of mines it is typically argued that the existence of a fixed stock of *in situ* mineral in the individual mine means that present and future production are necessarily antagonistic. That is, that physical depletion involves economic depletion.

The question of whether or not physical depletion does, indeed, involve economic depletion is one which can be shown to be inextricably bound up with the nature of return in mining over historical time and a major objective of this chapter is to investigate the nature of this return. It is, however, first necessary to undertake a discussion of the general nature of each of the various types of return which are identified in the literature of economics to see how each relates to the mineral industries. This general discussion of the particular nature of each type of return can then be used as the basis for an analysis of the way in which the interrelationships between them affects the overall nature of return over historical time and thus affects the relationship between physical and economic depletion.

As well as offering an analysis of the nature of historical return, this chapter also discusses the particular nature of short run return in mining. The nature of mining is such that it displays short run returns having characteristics which, if they are not peculiar to this industry, are at least prominent in it. This particular aspect of returns in mining is related to the effects of cumulative production and is one which is typically not addressed in discussions of the nature of return in general since it is not usually of great significance in agriculture or in manufacturing - the two great industries in which modern economics has been engrossed since its inception and at which the major part of the literature dealing with the nature of returns has been directed.[2] This particular aspect of return involves the inevitability, as production occurs, of significant, economically irreversible changes in the characteristics of at least some of the factor inputs. In the literature of mineral economics these changes are linked to the increasing depth at which accessible mineral must be mined as the contents of the mine are depleted. Now, at this stage, the reader might object that the nature of short run return is such that, by definition, no change may occur in the characteristics of the factor inputs employed and that, therefore, the changes which accompany depletion cannot relate to the short run. The question of whether or not this objection is valid is one which will be addressed at a later stage in this chapter. However, it may be noted here that the approach taken throughout this work is to follow the convention in the literature of treating the *in situ* mineral deposit as the fixed factor. The approach is thus one which considers the short run as involving the possibility of applying various quantities of variable factors to a fixed factor which is constituted by the *in situ* mineral deposit.

In this matter and in all others relating to return, this chapter does not involve any attempt to promote an alternative framework to the existing one in which the nature of returns is typically analysed; nor does it involve any attempt to redefine extant terms. Rather, it is simply directed at indicating how an understanding of the literature of mineral economics may be facilitated by a better understanding of its treatment of the nature of returns. It does, however, involve the introduction of a term which will be used to describe the effect of cumulative extraction upon return.

The next section of this chapter involves an overview of the general nature of the various types of return identified in the literature and relates them to the mineral industries. This overview forms the basis for a discussion of the nature of return observed over historical time which will be explained as involving the interaction of the various types of return identified in the overview. The particular nature of short run return in the mineral industries is then discussed and this discussion is followed by some concluding remarks.

The General Nature of Return

In the writings of the classical economists, the treatment of returns reveals that there are three distinct types of return which may be readily identified. The first of these to be considered here is the nature of *return on the extensive margin*. This return relates to the shift outwards of the extensive margin of agriculture and is associated with growth in real national income which is usually accompanied by population growth. It is a concept which typically relates to returns experienced over historical time.

In spite of the optimism of the populationists who believed that increasing population would be associated with increasing per capita income, the idea that as population increases diminishing returns will occur since increasingly inferior agricultural lands must be brought under cultivation was readily assimilated into the writings of the classical economists and was, with few exceptions, characteristic of them.[3] This pessimistic view which is most often associated with the names Malthus and Ricardo was challenged by a small number of classical economists, the most prominent of them being the American H.C. Carey. He argued that factors such as historical growth in technology and in the stock of capital would lead to the unlocking of resources superior to those currently in use giving increasing return over historical time.[4]

Recognizing the validity of the Carey argument, a few of the later classical economists and many of their neoclassical successors argued that over historical time either of the pessimistic or optimistic scenarios might occur - the former being more prominent in an old country, the latter more so in new countries. However, in spite of this acceptance of the possibility of increasing return on the extensive margin of agriculture and in spite of the suggestion by some of the classical economists that mining may often experience a similar increasing return, the contemporary theoretical literature of mineral economics emphasises the likelihood of decreasing return as extension of the margin involves the taking up of increasingly inferior resources.

The second type of return which may be identified in the writings of the classical economists is that which relates to the *intensive margin* and which involves a situation described in the modern literature as the short run - a situation characterised by the fixity of at least one of the factor services involved in production. Consideration of the nature of returns on the intensive margin eventually gave rise to the most famous of the laws of economics - the law of diminishing returns (of variable proportions). Although it is not necessary to reiterate the law here or to elaborate on the conditions under which it holds (those involving fixity of a factor service, homogeneity of the variable factor service and constancy of technical knowledge) it is important to note that the law entails that diminishing returns will occur eventually and that initial applications of the variable factor service may be associated with increasing or constant returns.

The third of the concepts of return which may be distilled from the writings of the classical economists is that associated with *technological change*. This type of return which is universally considered to be increasing is, unlike short run return but like the return on the extensive margin, typically examined in the context of the passage of historical time. As defined here and as it is typically defined, this return relates only to upward shifts in the short run total product curve (and to possible changes in its shape) and does not relate to technological change which, through its effect on the way in which the extensive margin is extended, affects the nature of returns on this margin. In fact, the convention of restricting returns to technological change to those which affect the nature of short run return is nowhere better exemplified than in the numerous cases where the significance of returns to technological change is indicated by considering their fortuitous tendency to counter, over historical time, the diminishing returns which are said to accompany the shift outwards of the extensive margin.[5]

Although some optimists saw the increasing returns which go with technological change as being supplemented by a tendency to increasing return on the extensive margin as increasingly superior resources were taken up, the welfare of mankind was more often seen to be the result of a tug-of-war between the opposing forces of diminishing return on the extensive margin and increasing return associated with technological change. Certainly, this is the context in which the mineral industries are typically analysed in the contemporary literature.

The last of the concepts of return to be discussed in the context of this general review is one which has its origins identified more with the work of neoclassical economists than with their classical predecessors. This is the concept of *returns to scale* which may relate to the scale of the firm or the industry. The concept of returns to scale of the firm is perhaps best understood by comparing it with the aforementioned short run returns. Whereas short run returns are those relevant to a situation in which at least one factor service is fixed in quantity, returns to scale of the firm are those which are relevant to the long run when all factor services may be varied. Although the emphasis in the literature is on the various scales of manufacturing plant or organisation which may be chosen in the long run, the concept is, of course, relevant to all productive activities including mining. As with short run returns, returns to scale or long run returns are often considered in a framework which abstracts from the passage of historical time - although empirical growth in the scale of production units over historical time has often been noted and analysed in the literature.[6] The nature of these returns may be such as to involve increasing, decreasing or constant return as the scale of the production unit is increased from any given size.

The convention in the literature of treating the mineral deposit as the short run fixed factor has as its corollary a long run which is characterised by the possibility of variation in the size of the *in situ* mineral deposit employed. Thus an analysis of long run returns may compare returns in the mine involving extraction from a large *in situ* deposit with those relating to extraction from a small deposit. The nature of these returns is related to the scale of the deposit. However, returns to scale may also relate to the scale of the mining organisation - their nature being revealed, for example, by a comparison of firms controlling a number of mines of given size with those controlling a different number of mines of similar size.

As well as relating to the scale of the firm, returns to scale may also be considered in relation to the scale of the industry as a whole. Whereas the concept of returns to scale of the firm relates to internal economies, returns to scale of the industry relate to external economies. That is, the firm may experience a change in its returns as a result of changes in the size of the industry in which it operates, *cet. par.*

Having discussed the four different types of return which are readily identified in the literature, the next section considers the particular relevance of each for mining in the context of the passage of historical time.

Mining Return in the Context of Historical Change

As indicated in the introductory remarks, this investigation is concerned, *inter alia*, with the way in which the nature of returns experienced over historical time in mining bears upon the relationship between physical and economic depletion. Although it is possible to conceive of a situation in place and in time which involves increasing, constant or diminishing return over historical time as short run output varies, the relationship between physical and economic depletion is, as the following discussion will indicate, independent of the nature of short run return. Thus the types of return relevant to this discussion are:

a) returns on the extensive margin,
b) returns to technological change, and
c) returns to scale.

An understanding of the way in which these types of return are interrelated in the context of the passage of historical time will be facilitated by considering each in turn.[7]

Returns on the Extensive Margin

Over historical time, mineral output may come from newly developed deposits for a number of reasons. *Cet. par.*, new mines may be opened as a consequence of one or a number of the following factors: i) In the face of increased demand, short run diminishing return dictates that increased output (per period) cannot be got from existing mines at lower cost than it can be obtained from new mines, ii) economic exhaustion of existing mines taken with the dictates of short run diminishing return prompts the opening of new mines, and iii) new mines which have lesser cost than some (or all) existing mines are discovered independently of causative factors such as i) and ii).[8]

Factors i) and ii) above may involve increasing, constant or decreasing return while iii) must involve increasing returns. If the need to open new mines as a consequence of factors i) and ii) above means the development of new mines involving inferior resources to those already in use, then the extensive margin is associated with diminishing returns.[9] If, on the other hand, the resources which are taken up as a result of factors i) and ii) are superior to some or all of those currently in use, then increasing returns prevail.

It is important to understand that increasing returns associated with the development of new, high return mines which involve exploitation of superior deposits does not imply irrational behaviour on the part of mining firms which currently operate old mines having lower return associated with the exploitation of inferior resources. These firms behaved rationally by choosing the resources which were superior at the time their mines were opened.[10] Since that time, however, the rank ordering of deposits has altered in such a way as to move the deposits which were once superior to lower rank as new, superior deposits have come into production. It is also important to understand that, in this case, the superiority of the new deposits is not caused by their having high return because they are at an early stage of exploitation while existing mines involve deposits which are nearing exhaustion and thus have a low return. In other words, the ranking of deposits is here based on the quality of the deposits as indicated by their average return over the life of the mine.

The causes of changes in the rank order of mineral deposits are many and varied; however, amongst those most often cited in the literature are discovery of new deposits, growth associated externalities (especially those related to transport), growth in the capital stock (both private and public) and technological changes in exploration, mining, processing and transport.[11] Now, in order to change the rank order of deposits these technological and other changes must be those which advantage some deposits in relation to others rather than those which reduce costs more or less proportionately for all deposits. It is technological changes which affect all deposits which are discussed in the next section.

Returns to Technological Change

As indicated above, returns to technological change are universally considered to be increasing and, as Schumpeter points out, there is no law of decreasing return to technological change.[12] That is, the upward shifts in the short run total product curves which occur with technological progress are not likely to become smaller and smaller over time.[13]

In relation to mining, increasing returns to technological change have been of great significance over the past two centuries, involving factors such as changes in the technologies of extraction, mineral processing and transport.[14] These technological changes are clearly similar to those which may be responsible for changes in the ranking of resources and which bring with them increasing return on the extensive margin. It might be argued, therefore, that there is no need to differentiate between technological change which gives increasing return on the extensive margin by altering the ranking of mineral deposits and technological change which gives increasing return by increasing the productivity of all deposits without altering their ranking. After all, in each case there is an increase in the ratio of output to input and in reality it may be difficult, if not impossible, to separate out the effects of technological changes which give increasing return on the extensive margin from those which give increasing return but do not affect the extensive margin.

Although, in reality, it may be difficult to distinguish between the two sources of increasing return which accompany technological change, it is important for heuristic purposes to separate them conceptually. While the reasons for this will be fully explained shortly when the interrelationship between various aspects of return is discussed, it is important to state at this stage that, although each of the two sources of increasing return associated with technological change will, *cet. par.*, affect mineral *output prices*, increasing return associated with changes in the way in which the extensive margin shifts out may alter the relative ranking of mineral deposits and may thus also affect mineral *deposit values*.[15] The term 'returns to technological change' is therefore used here to describe those returns to technological change which result from upward shifts in total product curves but not those which relate to the way in which the extensive margin shifts out. Aspects of technological change which are responsible for changes on the extensive margin - which change the ranking of deposits - are here taken to be part of the return on the extensive margin.

Returns to scale which may similarly be conceived of as having effects both on the extensive margin and within it are discussed in the next section.

Returns to Scale

Although returns to scale are often considered independently of the progress of historical time, empirical observation reveals that in mining in particular, there is a tendency for the scale of plant having greatest return at any time to increase over time and for growth in the size of a mineral industry to generate external economies. These increasing returns occur, in some cases, as a result of technological change (for example, the development of open cut techniques in the case of the firm or of bulk handling techniques for the industry) but in other cases the nature of return is independent of technological change, relating, for example, to factors such as specialisation of capital and labour in the firm or the development of infrastructure used by the industry.[16]

Like returns to technological change, returns to scale are, for heuristic purposes, here considered to have no role in the determination of the nature of the return on the extensive margin. That is, any effect that changes in scale may have upon the way in which the extensive margin shifts out are here taken to be part of the return on the extensive margin. In this way, the return on the extensive margin which affects both mineral output prices *and* mineral deposit values can be separated conceptually from returns to scale which are here confined to those aspects of changes in scale which, while they do affect mineral output prices, do not influence mineral deposit values.[17]

Having discussed the various aspects of return which are significant in the context of the passage of historical time, their interdependent nature and its relevance for the relationship between physical and economic depletion can now be addressed.

The Relationship Between Physical and Economic Depletion

In the modern theoretical literature dealing with the economics of mineral extraction, the mineral industries are typified as displaying decreasing return on the extensive margin and increasing return with respect to technological change and to scale. That is, assuming relatively stable demand, the progress of mineral output prices over time is said to be the outcome of the tug-of-war between decreasing return on the extensive margin which tends, *cet. par.*, to raise price over time and increasing returns to technological change and to scale which tend, *cet. par.*, to lower price over historical time. It is suggested that the relative strengths of the opposing teams in this tug-of-war are such that in the first half of this century real mineral output prices (across a number of industries) have remained relatively constant or perhaps have fallen.[18] If the net outcome of the interaction of each of the various aspects of return which is relevant to the progress of historical time is described as the *historical return*, then the progress of real mineral output prices over the first half of this century can be said to imply the existence of historically constant or increasing return.[19]

If it is assumed that returns to technological change and to scale are each always increasing over historical time (as is likely to be the case in reality - although this likelihood is not essential for the purpose of this theoretical discussion) then the inter-relationship between these two aspects of return and the third relevant aspect which involves the extensive margin can be discussed in a manageable yet meaningful way.

If, in a particular mineral industry, returns to technological change and to scale are increasing while returns on the extensive margin are decreasing, there are three possible outcomes in terms of the historical return experienced. Depending on the extent to which the diminishing return on the extensive margin is countered by the increasing returns to technological change and to scale, the resultant historical return may be decreasing, constant or increasing; implying that, with relatively stable demand, real mineral output prices will tend to rise, remain constant or fall respectively over historical time.[20]

Although real output prices may rise, remain constant or fall depending on the intensity of the decreasing return on the extensive margin in relation to the combined intensity of the increasing return to technological change and to scale, the existence of decreasing return on the extensive margin (recourse to inferior resources over time) means that *in situ* mineral resources are becoming scarcer over time. Mineral deposits above the margin and some of those below it will have capitalised values which tend to rise over time and which reflect the superiority of these resources over those to which resort must eventually be had;

those which are marginal in time. Thus, if there is decreasing return on the extensive margin, *in situ* mineral deposits will have capitalised values which will tend to rise over time regardless of the progress of mineral output prices.[21] The fact that certain *in situ* mineral deposits will have a capitalised value if returns on the extensive margin are decreasing means that physical depletion of these deposits reduces their value; that is, that physical depletion involves economic depletion or a user cost. These are high user cost exhaustible resources.

If, on the other hand, there are increasing returns on the extensive margin which reinforce the increasing returns to technological change and to scale, only a situation of historically increasing return can prevail and, assuming relatively stable demand, real mineral output prices will tend to fall over time. Furthermore, the presence of increasing return on the extensive margin (involving progression to superior resources over time) means, *cet. par.*, that *in situ* mineral deposits are becoming more abundant over time. The deposits which are currently being worked are the marginal deposits which have lower return than those which, although they are currently unworked, will be worked in the future as changes bring them above the current margin of production. The future development of mines having greater return than those currently being worked may bring with it the abandoning of existing mines; and the abandoning of these mines will occur for reasons other than their physical exhaustion or their encountering decreasing return as depths increase. That is, the development over historical time of new mines having greater return than those currently being worked may lead to the obsolescence and subsequent abandoning of the latter mines.[22]

If mines are operating in an environment in which their economic life is expected to be determined by obsolescence, then physical depletion of the mine may not be synonymous with economic depletion. The contents of the mine might have no capitalised value and extraction of ore from it might not involve user cost.[23] Minerals of this type are low or zero user cost exhaustible resources.

Although the finite nature of mineral deposits taken with the inevitability of physical depletion which accompanies production may suggest that a regime involving increasing abundance of mineral resources over time is unlikely, it is a possibility which has been suggested by some of the prominent economists to be reviewed in this study including Adam Smith, Henry Carey and

Gustav Cassel. In spite of the optimism of these authors, an examination of the history of the development of the economic treatment of mineral extraction over the past century reveals that by far the largest part of the literature has been produced during times of perceived natural resource crises and that the bulk of this literature, reflecting the pessimism of the times, has emphasised a high user cost of extraction associated with decreasing return on the extensive margin - any observed fall in real output prices being explained as a result of the increasing returns to technological change and to scale. Had the bulk of the literature been produced during the extensive periods in recent history when the availability of natural resources has been of less concern, it is likely that the optimistic possibility of increasing return on the extensive margin would have been more widely canvassed. This aspect is further considered in the conclusion to this book.

To suggest the possibility of increasing mineral abundance associated with increasing return on the extensive margin is not to imply that this is necessarily the normal state of affairs for all or even most mineral industries. If, however, certain mineral industries do, at certain times, display an ongoing tendency to increasing return on the extensive margin then this is of considerable significance for policy makers - especially in so far as matters such as depletion allowances, royalties and taxes are concerned. In the next section, the particular nature of short run return in mining is discussed.

Short Run Return in Mining

As is the case in the theoretical literature dealing with many other branches of industry, in the theoretical mineral economics literature the question of the nature of short run return is one which is typically no longer addressed - it being tacitly assumed that the law of diminishing return applies. However, in the early literature of mineral economics, the question of the nature of short run return in mining is one which was debated extensively and, as later chapters will show, it was not until the early part of this century that there was unanimous acceptance of the inevitability of short run diminishing return.

The fact that debate about the nature of short run return in mining continued long after acceptance of the inevitability of diminishing return in agriculture is testimony to the particular problems associated with analysing short run return in mining. As earlier stated, the convention in the literature is to treat the *in situ* mineral deposit as the short run fixed factor; and the origins of this tradition can be traced to the work of the classical economists. This convention is consistent with the treatment of the farm plot as the fixed factor in agriculture and, given the customs and institutions of modern capitalist economies, it can be seen to reflect, *inter alia*, the relative difficulty associated with changing the quantity of the natural resource factor employed as compared to changes in quantities of other factors inputs. Although the choice of the *in situ* mineral as the fixed factor is a logical one, it brings with it certain conceptual problems which have their foundation in the inescapable need to deplete this fixed factor as production occurs.

The traditional treatment of short run production theory involves, by assumption, the existence of a fixed productive factor service, and it might be thought that the depletion of the *in situ* deposit which must necessarily accompany production invalidates any attempt to treat it as the fixed factor. However, reduction in the size of the fixed factor need not necessarily involve any diminution in quantity of factor service which in the *in situ* mineral provides. As long as the same quantity of factor service is available at any time, the extent of the durability of the fixed factor is in this context irrelevant.[24] In the case of an underground mine for which the *in situ* mineral is taken as the fixed factor, the factor service supplied will involve the provision of an exposed mineral surface (a coal face, for example) which may be worked by the variable factor inputs employed. In the short run, the amount of *in situ* mineral remaining behind the face is irrelevant for production relationships (and may, in reality, be unknown).[25] Nonetheless, there are certain problems associated with other aspects of the short run and these will now be discussed.

If the output being considered in the short run were mineral removed from the face to the mine mouth and if, as extraction proceeded, the distance of the face from the mine mouth remained constant while the characteristics of the face were unchanging (in terms of surface area, quality of mineral, ease of removal, etc.) then the nature of the fixed and variable factor services may remain sufficiently unchanged, as extraction proceeds, to allow some sort of rigorous theoretical analysis of short run production akin to that of the textbooks. However, in reality, distance of the mineral face from the mine mouth does change with cumulative production as does the nature of the face itself. Although changes in the nature of the mineral face which accompany extraction may be satisfactorily accommodated in a theoretical analysis by the use of an appropriate simplifying assumption, the fact that extraction involves the inevitability of increasing distance of the mineral face from the mine mouth presents a more serious problem. Not only does increasing distance of the mineral face from the mine mouth mean that mineral output and some variable inputs must travel greater distances, it may also involve the need to prevent ingress of water, to provide stronger roof supports and so on. A knowledge of these and other associated factors has prompted economists to argue that mines are typically subject to decreasing return as cumulative production increases, *cet. par.*

The decreasing returns associated with cumulative production are clearly not short run diminishing returns - even though they relate to production in a situation which is characterized by fixity of the *in situ* mineral and which is described as the short run. These returns are more akin to returns on the extensive margin than to short run returns involving, as they do, an outward (or downward) shift in the margin of production in the mine which occurs as newly exposed mineral faces are removed sequentially. (Although economists have emphasised decreasing return as cumulative production increases, the return may be increasing if, for example, access to a superior mineral may be gained only by first mining an inferior one.)

While the return associated with cumulative production is akin to a return on the extensive margin, the peculiarities of mining mean that it is not identical to this return as it has been defined here and as it is typically defined in the literature. The difference between the two relates to the necessity for production from different quality resources to occur sequentially in the mine. In the mining *industry* (or in agriculture), production can occur simultaneously on both inferior and superior tracts. In the case of the individual mine, however, if removal of mineral of a given quality is a prerequisite to the removal of that of a different quality then both inferior and superior resources cannot be mined simultaneously.[26] Furthermore, any attempt to classify the return associated with cumulative production as a return on the extensive margin would mean that the short run would have to be characterised by a fixed factor involving only a small part of the *in situ* mineral deposit - an exposed mine face for example; and this would mean a break from the tradition of treating the *in situ* deposit as the fixed factor. As has already been indicated, it is not intended to break with that tradition here.

Although the question of the way in which the return associated with cumulative production might be classified is one which lies outside the scope of this chapter, it is, nonetheless, convenient at this stage to introduce a term which can be used in this work to describe changes in physical return which relate to changes in the extent of physical depletion of the contents of the mine. This term is *return to cumulative extraction*.

The inevitability of continuous change in the location of the mine face which occurs as production proceeds suggests that mineral production does not fit easily into the conventional model of short run production. This argument is even more compelling when the change in the nature of the capital input which occurs as production proceeds is taken into account. Not only is the 'fixed' factor service altered each time the mineral face is removed to reveal a new face, but the quantity of the capital input services also changes.

The removal of mineral on the mine face creates a space in which labour and capital may be located such that removal of the next face is facilitated. That is, the mining process creates an internal economy by the creation of a tunnel or hole which gives access to unmined mineral and an exit route for mineral output. The tunnel or hole which is so created forms part of the capital input and the removal of each mineral face using variable inputs of capital and labour involves the production of both mineral output *and* capital input.[27]

While this type of production process is not confined to mining, it remains that it is prominent in mining and that so long as the *in situ* deposit continues to be treated as the fixed factor there will be problems associated with the theoretical analysis of short run production using the conventional model.[28] Although, given certain simplifying assumptions, these problems may conceivably be accommodated by a complex dynamic production model, the need for such an approach may be obviated, in some instances, by a simpler device. Rather than considering the nature of short run return in relation to the rate at which a small part of the output of the mine is produced and in so doing having to accommodate the problem of the changing nature of return as cumulative production increases, an approach involving the examination of return in relation to the rate at which the whole of the contents of the mine are extracted is one which will, *cet. par.*, reveal the nature of return at various output rates while the effect of cumulative production on return remains constant.[29] This is the technique which Alfred Marshall employed when considering the question of whether mines, like agricultural lands, display short run diminishing returns:

> '[M]ines are as it were nature's reservoir. The more nearly a reservoir is exhausted, the greater is the labour of pumping from it but if one man could pump it out in ten days, ten men could pump it out in one day: and when once empty, it would yield no more. So the mines that are being opened this year might just as easily have been opened many years ago: if the plans had been properly laid in advance, and the requisite specialized capital and skill got ready for the work, ten year's supply of coal might have been raised in one year without any increased difficulty; and when a vein had once given up its treasure, it could produce no more.'[30]

Although Marshall does not give any reason for considering short run return in the mine in relation to the whole rather than part of its contents, he presumably saw that his purpose was admirably suited by an approach which effectively neutralised the complications involved in asking whether mines display short run diminishing return at any particular stage of their life. While an approach which neutralizes these complications will be appropriate in some contexts, in others the requirement will be for a more complex approach in which identification of the nature and extent of the return to cumulative extraction is essential. However, questions of the type of model in which the particular nature of short run return might best be analysed lie outside the scope of this chapter which is concerned only with identifying and explaining the relevance of aspects of the conventional treatment of return in mining. This having been done it is necessary only to make some concluding remarks.

Conclusion

In considering the general nature of return in mining, this chapter has emphasised two particular aspects of return. The first of these is the return on the extensive margin which has been shown to be of particular relevance for the determination of mineral deposit values and thus for the relationship between economic and physical depletion. Although the contemporary literature dealing with the economics of mineral extraction emphasises cases of decreasing return on the extensive margin where physical and economic depletion are synonymous, as this chapter has shown, recognition of the possibility of increasing return on the extensive margin introduces the prospect of there being little or no user cost associated with the physical depletion of the contents of the mine; and it need not be inferred from the emphasis given to the decreasing return case in the contemporary literature that cases of increasing return are of little practical significance. Just as the dismal science gains greatest prominence in economically troubled times, so the literature of the economics of mineral extraction shows greatest growth in times of perceived resource crises when the pessimistic case of decreasing return on the extensive margin is most apparent.[31] Had the economics of mineral extraction been a more fashionable topic during the relatively long periods in recent history when the natural resource outlook has been more optimistic, the tenor of this literature is likely to have been very different.

The second aspect of return to be given prominence in this chapter is short run return which has been shown to be more complex in the case of the mine than it is in many other productive activities. Although this complexity - which relates to changes which occur with cumulative production - does not pose any fundamental theoretical problems, it does create difficulties in so far as practical explanation and application of short run theoretical production relationships are concerned. The discussion of the nature of short run return in this chapter has addressed some of these practical problems by, firstly, indicating their nature and, secondly, suggesting ways in which they may be accommodated. Finally, the reader is reminded that the primary purpose of this chapter has been to provide a background to the nature of mining return which will facilitate an understanding of the review of authors which follows in Part II of this work.

Notes

1. W.R. Sorley, 'Mining royalties and their effect on the iron and coal trades', *Royal Statistical Society Journal*, vol. 52 (1889), p. 74. Sorley's contribution to the literature is discussed in chapter 10 below.

2. This is not to deny the existence of investigations into the nature of return in industries such as transport, power generation, oil refining and so on.

3. The circumstances leading to the triumph of the pessimistic Malthusian view over the optimism of the populationists is well summarized by Schumpeter. J.A. Schumpeter, *History of Economic Analysis* (George, Allen and Unwin, London, 1954), pp. 250-8.

4. Extensive discussion of Carey's hypothesis may be found in chapter 7 below.

5. J.S. Mill provides a good example of this approach in his *Principles* where he also notes that improvements in government and in social and moral advancement have similar effects to those of technological progress. J.S. Mill, *Principles of Political Economy* (Routledge, London, 1895), bk 1, ch. 12. In the context of the contemporary theoretical mineral economics literature, Solow's Ely Lecture also provides a good example of this approach. R.M. Solow, 'The economics of resources or the resources of economics', *American Economic Review,* vol. 64 (1974), pp. 1-4.

6. George Stigler's 'Survivor Principle' provides one of the best examples of analysis of change in the size of production units over historical time. G. Stigler, 'The economies of scale', *Journal of Law and Economics,* vol. 1, no. 1 (1958).

7. Although the analysis of each of the types of return discussed here is made manageable by considering each in a partial framework, it is acknowledged that this approach has some important limitations. A highly original discussion of some of the significant interdependencies which occur in the mineral industries but which are often neglected in the literature can be found in A. Fitzgibbons and S. Cochrane, 'Optimal rate of natural resource depletion', *Resources Policy,* vol. 4, no. 3 (1978). A brief resume of the seminal literature dealing with the overall nature of return in the firm and in the macro economy may be found in H.F. Breimeyer, 'Agriculture's three economies in a changing resource environment', *American Journal of Agricultural Economics,* vol. 60, no. 1 (1978).

8. In this context, the opening of 'new' mines may involve events such as the reopening of previously abandoned mines and the working of old tailings as well as the commencement of mines exploiting virgin deposits.

9. Inferiority (or superiority) of mineral resources may relate to a number of criteria including location, ore grade, depth below the earth's surface etc. Although, in the context of this discussion, *in situ* resources may occur in a range of qualities, it is assumed throughout that mineral output is homogeneous. Some of the pitfalls of carrying an assumption such as this over to the real world are considered in my 1979 note in *Energy Policy.* T.J.C. Robinson, 'The distinction between coking coal and steaming coal - implications for the assessment of energy resources', *Energy Policy,* vol. 7, no. 1 (1979).

10. A basic feature of the modern theoretical mineral economics literature is the idea that rational behaviour involves the exploitation of known mineral deposits in order of return - commencing with the deposit having highest return, *cet. par.* See, for example, Solow, 'The economics of resources or the resources of economics'.

11. Changes involving transport may well be the most important contributor to alteration of the ranking of deposits over time. Not only will the development of new modes and new routes be significant in this regard but so will reduction in transport cost for existing modes on existing routes. In relation to this last aspect, the marked decline in bulk mineral shipping costs which occurred in the 1950s and 1960s was responsible for significant changes in ranking of deposits both within and between nations. An indication of the extent of this decline in costs may be found in T.J.C. Robinson, 'The costs of ocean transport of bulk minerals', *International Journal of Transport Economics,* vol. 4, no. 4 (1977), Table 3.

12. Schumpeter, *History,* p. 263. Blaug also makes this point. M. Blaug, *Economic Theory in Retrospect,* 2nd edn (Heinemann, London, 1968), pp. 71-2.

13. Indeed, if the beneficial effects of ongoing technological change grow exponentially - as the new technology builds on the old - then an hypothesis of increasing return to technological change may be warranted. 'Thus change becomes progressive and propagates itself in a cumulative way.' A.A. Young, 'Increasing returns and economic progress', *Economic Journal*, vol. 38 (1928), p. 535.

14. The contemporary significance of technological change for return in mining is well summarised by Bosson and Varon and by McAllister. See R. Bosson and B. Varon, *The Mining Industry and the Developing Countries* (Oxford University Press, New York, 1977), pp. 34-7; and A.L. McAllister, 'Price technology and ore reserves' in G.J.S. Govett and M.H. Govett (eds), *World Mineral Supplies* (Elsevier, Amsterdam, 1976).

15. This assertion involves some heroic assumptions, the most important of which is the assumption that technological change which increases return but does not alter ranking has no effect on mineral deposit values. Relaxation of this assumption would not alter the conclusions drawn in this chapter although it would certainly make the analysis much more complex.

16. A succinct resume of the sources of, and the significance of, returns to scale in mining can be found in Bosson and Varon, *The Mining Industry*, pp. 34-7.

17. The heroic assumptions alluded to in note 15 above apply equally here.

18. See H.J. Barnett and C. Morse, *Scarcity and Growth* (Resources for the Future, Baltimore, 1963), ch. 8 and Bosson and Varon, *The Mining Industry*, pp. 113-17.

19. Although Schumpeter reserves the term *historical return* for the return to technological progress, in common usage it describes the net outcome of the interaction of the various aspects of return which are relevant to the passage of historical time. The latter meaning is the one given to the term by Blaug in his *Economic Theory in Retrospect*. Schumpeter, *History*, pp. 262-3 and Blaug, *Economic Theory*, p. 191. The statement that constant or falling real prices imply constant or increasing return is one in which it is assumed firstly, that prices are cost based and secondly, that cost and return are opposite sides of the same coin. Although the validity of the first of these assumptions may be questioned, the second has the imprimatur of J.A. Schumpeter who argues that it constitutes a 'bad habit' which does not, as far as he is aware, involve any error. Schumpeter, *History*, p. 1045n. This implied correspondence between real prices and physical return also involves the realistic assumption that a constant or downward secular trend in real prices is not the result of decreasing demand over time.

20. The assumptions discussed in note 19 above also apply here.

21. It is implicit in this statement that the regime of decreasing return on the extensive margin is expected to be ongoing. The heroic assumptions alluded to in note 15 above are also relevant here.

22. Writing about the demise of the copper and tin mines of Cornwall in the last half of the nineteenth century, L.H. Courtney noted the occurrence of events such as those described here. Outlining the enormous increase in British consumption of imported copper in relation to local production he states that 'this great change has not been due to any absolute exhaustion of copper mines at home, but to the relatively greater cheapness of production elsewhere.' Similarly, in relation to tin mining he notes that '[t]he cheapness of production elsewhere, chiefly in the East, has caused the abandonment of mines that might otherwise have remained in working, the survivors alone being able to stand the competition which threatens the existence of almost every one of them'. L.H. Courtney, 'Jevons's Coal Question: thirty years after', *Royal Statistical Society Journal*, vol.

15, no. 4 (1897), pp. 807-8. Other practical examples of this process are discussed in the conclusion to this work.

23. Whether the contents of a particular mine will have a capitalised value under these circumstances will depend, *inter alia*, on the timing of the opening of new, superior mines and the extent of their superiority, as well as the relative quality of other extant mines and the timing of their closure.

24. A different example of a non-durable factor providing a fixed factor service may help to clarify this point. In a particular smelting industry, a short run production model may be developed in which successive charges of coal, for example, provide a constant quantity of heat per time period; and this constant quantity of heat will constitute the fixed factor service with which various quantities of variable factor services may be combined. In this case, the quantity of heat input per time period (the fixed factor service) may be held constant although the non-durable coal input must continually be replenished.

25. H.S. Gordon's criticism of Alfred Marshall's treatment of short run diminishing returns in fishing makes the same point in relation to fishing as is being made here in relation to mining; namely, that production itself alters the nature of the production process. Although Gordon correctly identifies the general nature of the problems associated with short run production processes where production itself causes changes in the production process by changing the nature of factor inputs, in so doing he incorrectly asserts that exposition of the law of diminishing returns requires an assumption that the size of the natural resource factor is constant. His paper concludes with the statement that the law of diminishing return is 'theoretically incompatible with any statement concerning changes in the size of the natural resource.' H.S. Gordon, 'On a misinterpretation of the law of diminishing returns in Marshall's *Principles*', *Canadian Journal of Economics*, vol. 18 (1952), in J.C. Wood (ed.), *Alfred Marshall : Critical Assessments*, vol. 3 (Croom Helm, London, 1982), pp. 263-5. On the relationship between factor services and the factors which provide them see: G.J. Stigler, *The Theory of Price* (Macmillan, New York, 1950), pp. 114-5.

26. An economic rather than physical impediment to simultaneous mining is implied here.

27. As well as this inevitable increase in capital which accompanies the production of output, there is also likely to be a discretionary increase in capital in the form of roof supports, rails, conveyors, etc.

28. Almost all production processes will involve some inevitable changes in the nature of factor inputs as production occurs - although in many cases the changes will be relatively insignificant. Productive activities other than mining in which these changes are of particular significance include road and railway construction, the construction of multi-storey buildings etc. Each of these activities is characterised by an economic (and, in some cases, physical) need for production to occur sequentially in a manner which causes a marked and economically irreversible change in the nature of some of the intensively used factor inputs.

29. For theoretical purposes, the whole of the contents of the mine will mean the whole of the economically exploitable - as opposed to physical - contents.

30. A. Marshall, *Principles of Economics,* 8th edn, 1949 resetting (Macmillan, London, 1920), p. 139.

31. The perceived resource crises of recent history have occurred in the United States around the turn of the century, and world wide in the 1970s.

Part II : The Economics of Exhaustible Resources

4

Adam Smith

Adam Smith's wide ranging treatment of British industry in the *Wealth of Nations* includes an extensive discussion of the mineral industries; and this discussion may well have prompted similar consideration of mining by later classical writers such as Ricardo, Mill and Marx.

Although, according to Young's estimate, the mining, metallurgy, building and hardware industries contributed in total just eleven percent of British national income in 1770, mining is nonetheless given thorough treatment by Smith.[1] His discussion includes consideration of coal mining, tin mining and quarrying in the British Isles as well as the exploitation of precious metals and precious stones in other parts of the world. The major part of Smith's discussion of mining is undertaken in his chapter dealing with the rent of land[2] - although there is some discussion of the mining of precious metals included in his analysis of the determination of the nominal price of commodities.[3]

The genesis of Smith's thorough treatment of mining lies in his desire to distinguish land which produces food and which always affords a rent from land (including mines) which produces the materials of clothing, lodging and equipage and which may or may not afford a rent. Smith argues that as a result of growth in population and the associated increase in industrial activity, it might be expected that the produce (including minerals) of land which may or may not afford a rent will become progressively dearer and dearer in relation to food.[4] However, there are factors which will tend to mitigate this effect including discovery of new lands, technological change and positive externalities associated with growth. In discussing these mitigating effects Smith provides the basis for an essentially optimistic view of the availability of mineral resources. Smith's discussion of mines combines, in characteristic fashion, both static and dynamic analyses and the demarcation of these approaches is, *inter alia*, one of the major goals of this chapter.[5]

This chapter commences with a general, descriptive discussion of Smith's treatment of the rent of mines. This discussion provides the basis for the second part of the chapter which explores the analytical content of Smith's treatment. Finally, some conclusions are drawn.

The Rent of Mines

The second part of Adam Smith's chapter dealing with the rent of land considers the produce of land which sometimes does and sometimes does not afford a rent. This part is devoted primarily to a discussion of the mineral industries. In discussing mines, Smith takes the recurring classical view that the price of the output of the industry must be sufficient to replace the stock with ordinary profits of the highest cost mine - costs being determined by both fertility and situation:

'There are some of which the produce is barely sufficient to pay the labour, and replace, together with its ordinary profits, the stock employed in working them. They afford some profit to the undertaker of the work, but no rent to the landlord. They can be wrought advantageously by nobody but the landlord, who being himself undertaker of the work, gets the ordinary profit of the capital which he employs in it. Many coal-mines in Scotland are wrought in this manner and can be wrought in no other. The landlord will allow nobody else to work them without paying some rent, and nobody can afford to pay any.

Other coal-mines in the same country sufficiently fertile, cannot be wrought on account of their situation. A quantity of mineral sufficient to defray the expence of working, could be brought from the mine by the ordinary, or even less than the ordinary quantity of labour: But in an inland country, thinly inhabited, and without either good roads or water-carriage, this quantity could not be sold.'[6]

And further:

'The lowest price at which coals can be sold for any considerable time, is, like that of all other commodities, the price
which is barely sufficient to replace, together with its ordinary
profits, the stock which must be employed in bringing them
to market. At a coal-mine for which the landlord can get no
rent, but which he must either work himself or let it alone
altogether, the price of coals must generally be nearly about
this price.'[7]

Unlike later authors such as Sorley and Marshall, Smith does
not consider the possibility that the marginal mine may, in the
normal course of events pay a rent or royalty.[8] However, Smith
does note that whereas the price of a mineral such as coal does
have an upper bound determined by the price of the substitute
wood, in the case of the precious metals the lack of a good
substitute means that there is no effective ceiling to their prices.[9]
The need to replace the stock with ordinary profits in the
highest cost mine is, however, only one element in the determination of the price of minerals. Smith lays great emphasis on the
role of the more abundant mines in the determination of price:

'The most fertile coal mine too, regulates the price of coals
at all the other mines in its neighbourhood.'[10]

And further:

'The price ... of the coarse, and still more that of the precious
metals, at the most fertile mines in the world, must necessarily more or less affect their price at every other in it.'[11]

This static analysis which emphasises the role of low cost mines in
determining the price of minerals at any time, is intertwined with
a dynamic factor involving the displacement of high cost mines by
lower cost mines. Discussing the role of the low cost coal mine
Smith says:

'Both the proprietor [of the most fertile mine] and the undertaker of the work find, the one he can get a greater rent, the
other that he can get a greater profit, by somewhat underselling all their neighbours. Their neighbours are soon

obliged to sell at the same price, though they cannot so well afford it, and though it always diminishes, and sometimes takes away altogether both their rent and their profit. Some works are abandoned altogether; others can afford no rent, and can be wrought only by the proprietor.'[12]

In discussing the precious metals he gives a practical example of the way in which the shift outward of the extensive margin may result in the displacement of high cost mines:

'After the discovery of the mines of Peru, the silver mines of Europe were, the greater part of them, abandoned. The value of silver was so much reduced that their produce could no longer pay the expense of working them, or replace, with a profit, the food, cloaths, lodging, and other necessaries which were consumed in that operation.'[13]

From the foregoing analysis of the nature of mines Smith argues that the rent of mines is generally lower than that of most other parts of the rude produce of land: 'Rent, accordingly, seems at the greater part of mines to have but a small share in the price of the coarse, and a still smaller in that of the precious metals.'[14] He cites numerous examples of the low rent of mines and of its diminution over time including the following:

'In the silver mines of Peru, ...the proprietor frequently exacts no other acknowledgement from the undertaker of the mine, but that he will grind the ore at his mill, paying him the ordinary multure or price of grinding.'[15]

Not only are rents low in the mineral industries but so too are profits since insufficient account is taken of risk:

'Mining, it seems, is considered [in Peru] in the same light as here, as a lottery in which the prizes do not compensate the blanks though the greatness of some tempt many adventurers to throw away their fortunes in such unprosperous projects.'[16]

Having comprehensively discussed mines as an example of land of the type which sometimes does and sometimes does not afford a rent, Smith goes on in the third part of his chapter on the rent of land to discuss the relationship between the price of produce of land which always affords a rent and the price of produce of land which sometimes does and sometimes does not afford a rent.

As outlined in the introduction to this chapter Smith felt that the forces of industrial progress and population growth would cause the prices of the produce of land other than food to rise relative to food prices. He says, however, that although this might be expected theoretically, certain historical accidents have meant that there are prominent cases where the opposite has occurred.[17] These historical accidents have meant that although progress and population growth have greatly increased the demand for certain commodities, greater increases in their supply have brought about falling rather than rising prices.

The example which Smith uses to illustrate his point is that of the world market for silver. He argues that in Europe the preceding four centuries were characterised by three stages in the development of the market for silver. In the first stage growing demand outstripped supply leading to a rise in the value of silver; in the second period supply increased for many years at a greater rate than demand resulting in a fall in price; and in the third period supply and demand increased at similar rates resulting in stable prices.[18]

Smith concludes his discussion of the produce of land which may or may not afford a rent by using his observations regarding variations in the price of silver as the basis for a long and detailed digression into the causes of these variations.[19] Although the details of this discussion of the evolution of the market for silver are of little relevance to this review of Smith, his conclusion to the section dealing with the third period (characterised by stable prices) is of more than passing interest. Smith concludes that because exploration is so uncertain there is an equal chance that over the next one or two centuries silver production will come from mines more fertile than the most fertile mines discovered to date or alternatively that it will come from mines more barren than those of antiquity.[20] In a direct refutation of Mercantilist doctrine he concludes that no matter which of these two possibilities occurs, the real wealth and prosperity of the world will be little affected.[21]

In discussing the rent of mines Smith offers a comprehensive analysis which involves the intertwining of both static and dynamic elements. In the next section of this chapter an attempt is made to unravel these elements so that an appraisal of his analytical contribution can be made.

Analysis of the Treatment of Mines

Throughout Smith's discussion of mines there are two major recurring themes. The first of these involves the idea that both the lowest cost and the highest cost mines have a role to play in regulating the price of mineral output. Smith's second theme relates to the phenomenon of the displacement of high cost mines by newly developed low cost mines. Although it will be argued later in this chapter that the first of these themes is perfectly consistent with the conventional, classical *static* approach to the determination of price in a *competitive* market, there are, however, alternative points of view which variously attribute Smith's inclusion of the low cost mine in the determination of price to the existence of *monopoly* elements or to the significance of *dynamic* factors.

The monopoly argument is put forward by Hollander who argues that '[m]onopoly power is manifested - and exerts itself - in the undercutting of less productive mines.'[22] Hollander goes on to quote the passage above in which Smith discusses the way in which more fertile coal mines undersell their neighbours forcing them in some cases to abandon their mines. (As will be seen in a later chapter, W.R. Sorley writing in the 1880s assigns a price determining role to the more fertile mine which he also attributes to monopoly power. He does not, however, cite Smith as a source of this attribution.) Whereas Hollander's monopoly explanation of Smith's role for the more fertile mine is offered in the context of a *static* interpretation of the determination of price, Schumpeter's interpretation of Smith's position involves a *dynamic* element.

In discussing the supposed contradiction between Smith's opinion that the lowest cost firm tends to regulate price and Ricardo's view that it is the highest cost firm which does so, Schumpeter argues that there is, in fact, no contradiction.[23] According to Schumpeter, Smith 'thought of the process by which more progressive firms crowd out less efficient ones and for a time force them to sell at losses. Ricardo described an equilibrium state.'[24] Schumpeter sees Smith's role for the more fertile mine as a temporary one. He says - in the quotation above - that the less efficient mines are forced to sell at losses 'for a time'. Clearly, Schumpeter is thinking of Smith's description as dynamic in the sense that it describes a passing disequilibrium state.[25]

Karl Marx also considered Smith's discussion of the important role for the intramarginal mine. He drew a similar conclusion to Schumpeter's, arguing that although Smith's idea that the more fertile mine normally regulates price is wrong, his analysis of those less common cases where the more fertile mine does regulate price is correct. Like Schumpeter, Marx attributes to Smith a *dynamic* view of the intrusion of low cost mines which involves falling output prices.[26] Contrary to Schumpeter's and to Marx's view, Alfred Marshall argues that although Smith's meaning is not clear he 'does not appear to be referring to any temporary underselling'.[27]

In drawing conclusions about Smith's role for the low cost mine in the determination of price, the authors who have been quoted above failed to interpret the relevance of his analysis of the international metals market for their arguments. Had they done so, they may have suggested an alternative explanation for the emphasis on the importance of the low cost mine - an explanation such as that which will now be suggested.

Discussing the role of the most fertile metal mines in the world Smith says:

'the productions of the most distant metallic mines frequently may, and in fact commonly are [brought into competition with each other].'[28]

And further:

'The price of copper in Japan must have some influence upon its price at the copper mines of Europe. The price of silver in Peru, or the quantity either of labour or of other goods which it will purchase there, must have some influence on its price, not only at the silver mines of Europe, but at those of China.'[29]

Smith follows this *static* analysis of existing conditions in the silver mining industry with a discussion of the *dynamic* process by which the discovery of the silver mines of Peru led to the abandoning of silver mines in Europe. That is, Smith's discussion of the abandoning of European mines as a result of the discoveries of Peru is an explanation of the *dynamic* process which led to the existing *static* conditions in the industry which are characterised by a role for both low cost and high cost mines in the determination of price.

If a modern, comparative static approach is applied to Smith's static analysis of the determination of metal prices it can be shown that in this context it is an unremarkable concept which sits easily within the accepted theoretical framework. In discussing the relevance of the lowest cost mine, Smith attributes to it a role in 'regulating' or 'affecting' price. He does so having already made it clear that mineral prices will approximate costs in the highest cost mine (the mine which is able to replace, with ordinary profits, its stock but which pays no rent). From a modern viewpoint Smith's role for the most fertile mine can be seen as one in which the size and degree of fertility of that mine affects the shape and position of the market supply curve and thus, *cet. par.*, affects the point of intersection of the market supply curve with the market demand curve. This conclusion may reasonably be inferred from the last two quotations above in which Smith argues that certain metal prices at any place in the world are typically a function of the world supply of these metals. That is, although market price must be sufficient to cover costs in the marginal mine, the determination of which mine will be the marginal mine is a function, *cet. par.*, of the size and cost structure of intramarginal mines. Buchanan, in editing the *Wealth of Nations* in 1814, put a similar construction on Smith's remarks regarding the role of the most fertile coal mines: 'It is not by the produce of one coal mine, however fertile, but by the joint produce of all the coal mines that can be worked, that the price of coals is fixed. A certain quantity of coals only can be consumed at a certain price. If the mines that can be worked produce more than this quantity the price will fall; if they produce less it will rise.'[30]

Smith's assertion that the most fertile as well as the least fertile mine 'regulates' price is thus seen to be consistent with static equilibrium in a competitive market. On the basis of this interpretation there is clearly no contradiction between Ricardo and Smith since both argue that price will approximate costs in the highest cost mine. However, Smith's analysis is the more comprehensive since he also considers the relevance of intramarginal mines in determining which will be the marginal mine.

In the introduction to this section dealing with the analytical content of Smith's treatment of the mineral industries it was pointed out that Smith pursued two recurring themes. The first of these, involving the *static* determination of price, has been discussed above. The second, which relates to the *dynamic* process through which low cost mines displace existing high cost mines will now be considered.

For Smith, the most obvious example of the displacement process is the effect of the discoveries of the silver mines of Peru upon the world silver market. His discussion of the ability of low cost coal mines to displace existing high cost mines may also be interpreted as an example of this dynamic process.[31] The concomitant of this displacement process is the relatively low rent afforded to existing mines which are not displaced by low cost mines but which, nonetheless, have their rent yielding capacity severely curtailed by competition from new, low cost mines.

Whereas, at any point in time, price will approximate costs in the highest cost mine, over time a dynamic process occurs in which existing, high cost mines are displaced by new, low cost mines. Smith notes that a similar dynamic process may occur in relation to agriculture. He argues that the prices of agricultural produce in the towns are reduced by improvements in transport (for example the building of roads and canals) which encourage cultivation of remote areas and thus provide increased competition to land adjacent to the towns.[32]

Although, in the case of agriculture, Smith attributes falling prices to technological progress in the form of improvements in transport modes, in the case of the world silver market he attributes falling prices to what he describes as the 'accidental' discoveries of the New World. Is it to be inferred from this description that he considers these discoveries to be unexpected events which are unlikely to occur again or, alternatively, as events which, although unexpected, have a high probability of occurring again? Unfortunately Smith gives a non-committal answer to this question. As was indicated above, in discussing the prospects for the world silver mining industry Smith argues that although the future may see the opening of highly fertile mines, on the other hand it is just as likely that only relatively infertile mines will be discovered. The intrusion of low cost mines into the market can thus be seen to result from accidental discoveries or, if inference can be drawn from Smith's treatment of agriculture, as a result of externalities generated by economic progress - for example, in the area of transport.

Conclusion

Adam Smith offers a comprehensive analysis of the mineral industries which, in typical fashion, draws heavily upon empirical evidence. Like other classical authors his treatment is also strongly supply oriented.

While Smith's *static* analysis reveals the conventional conclusion that prices will approximate costs in the marginal mine, it goes further than this to consider the role of low cost intramarginal mines in determining the position and shape of the short run supply curve; that is, the role of low cost mines in the determination of which mine will be the marginal mine. Smith's emphasis on the role of the low cost mine in his *static* analysis may be attributed to his understanding of the empirically observed *dynamic* process in which new low cost mines displace existing high cost mines. Although, as his analysis of the silver market shows, not all historical periods are characterised by the intrusion of low cost mines, conditions of increasing return on the extensive margin are sufficiently common in the mineral industries to be cited as the cause of the empirically observed tendency for rents to be low in these industries.

For the purposes of comparison with later authors it is important to understand at this stage that the conditions of historically decreasing cost which Smith observed in many mineral industries result from increasing return on the extensive margin involving a lower cost of exploiting new mines *vis-a-vis* existing mines rather than from a process of technological or other change which reduces costs for old mines and new mines alike. That is, Smith argued that the historically increasing returns observed in many mining industries were the result of changes, over time, in the rank ordering of deposits according to their relative production costs. Now, changes which involve reversal of the ranking of mineral deposits will, *cet. par.*, diminish the user cost of exploiting existing mines, whereas changes which reduce costs for all mines but do not alter their ranking will not, *cet. par.*, significantly alter the user cost of exploiting existing mines. In short, Smith observed a common tendency to historically increasing returns of a type which implies that mineral extraction involves relatively low or even zero user cost.

Notes

1. Quoted in S. Hollander, *The Economics of Adam Smith* (Heinemann, London, 1973), p. 108.

2. A. Smith, *An Inquiry into the Nature and Causes of the Wealth of Nations* (Methuen, London, 1904), vol. 1, bk 1, ch. 11. All future references are to this edition.

3. Ibid., ch. 5.

4. Ibid., pp. 175-6.

5. General discussion of Smith's use of static and dynamic analyses can be found in A. Skinner's introduction to the Penguin edition of *The Wealth of Nations* (Penguin, Harmondsworth, 1970), pp. 65-6 and in the introduction to the edition edited by R.H. Campbell, A.S. Skinner and W.B. Todd (Clarendon, Oxford, 1976), pp. 27-8.

6. Smith, *Wealth of Nations*, p. 166.

7. Ibid., p. 168.

8. See chapters 10 and 11 below.

9. Smith, *Wealth of Nations*, p. 172.

10. Ibid., p. 167.

11. Ibid., pp. 168-9.

12. Ibid., pp. 167-8.

13. Ibid., p. 169.

14. Ibid.

15. Ibid.

16. Ibid., pp. 170-1. In this regard, Smith's general discussion of the sanguinity of investors and the resultant overvaluation of the opportunity for profit is also relevant. See ibid., p. 109.

17. Ibid., pp. 175-6.

18. Ibid., bk 1, ch. 11, part 3.

19. Ibid.

20. Ibid., p. 236.

21. Ibid. As an aside, it is interesting to compare this conclusion with Keynes's opposite conclusion: 'At periods when gold is available at suitable depths experience shows that the real wealth of the world increases rapidly; and when but little of it is so available, our wealth suffers stagnation and decline.' J.M. Keynes, *The General Theory of Employment Interest and Money* (Macmillan, London, 1936), p. 130.

22. Hollander, *Adam Smith*, p. 166 *n*.

23. J.A. Schumpeter, *History of Economic Analysis* (George, Allen and Unwin), London, 1954, p. 673 *n*.

24. Schumpeter, ibid. J.U. Nef offers a similar explanation for Smith's emphasis on the low cost mine. See chapter 6 below where the contradiction between Smith and Ricardo regarding the determination of price is further discussed.

25. Schumpeter's definitions of statics and dynamics which he attributes to Ragnar Frisch may be found on page 936 of his *History*.

26. K. Marx, *Theories of Surplus Value* (Lawrence and Wishart, London, 1969), part II, pp. 339 and 364.

27. A. Marshall, *Principles of Economics*, 8th edn, 1949 resetting (Macmillan, London, 1920), p. 364 *n*.

28. Smith, *Wealth of Nations*, p. 168.

29. Ibid., p. 169. The Duke of Argyll was later to have first hand experience of the effects of competition from abroad and this led him to support Smith's idea that the least cost mine has a role in regulating price. The Duke's experiences are further discussed in the conclusion to this study.

30. Quoted in Smith, *Wealth of Nations*, p. 167 *n*.

31. Marx declares that Smith is correct in emphasising increasing return on the extensive margin in mining: 'Adam Smith makes a correct distinction here between land and mines, because with the latter he presupposes that there is *never* a transition to worse sorts - always to *better* ones - and that they always provide more than the necessary additional supply.' Marx, *Theories*, p. 338, original emphasis.

32. Smith, *Wealth of Nations*, pp. 148-9.

5

David Ricardo

There are three places in Ricardo's *Principles of Political Economy and Taxation* where analysis of the economics of mining is undertaken. The first, which appears in the chapter on rent, distinguishes the rent of mines from the rent of agricultural lands;[1] the context for this discussion being the inadequacy of Adam Smith's earlier consideration of rent. The second analysis of mines occurs in the short chapter on the rent of mines which has the primary purpose of providing the justification for the use of gold as an invariant measure of value.[2] This chapter also contains the famous contradictory reference to the rent of mines in which the restrictive definition of rent laid down in the previous chapter on rent is contravened. Contravention of this definition is also found in the third instance of analysis of the economics of mines which occurs in the chapter dealing with the doctrine of Adam Smith concerning the rent of land.[3] Analytical treatment of the economics of mining cannot be found elsewhere in Ricardo's works - although some of his parliamentary speeches do refer to conditions in the domestic coal trade.

Ricardo's analysis of the mineral industries is very different from that of Adam Smith; it is more analytical than descriptive and accords with the common view of Ricardo's writings as being difficult and contradictory.[4] Nevertheless, Ricardo has a significant and lasting contribution to make to the narrowly defined area of the economics of exhaustible resources.

The first part of this chapter involves a discussion of Ricardo's sometimes puzzling analysis of the rent of mines. This discussion is followed by consideration of his more general treatment of the mineral industries after which some conclusions are drawn.

The Rent of Mines

Ricardo's first reference to mines in the *Principles* is made in the introductory chapter dealing with rent. Ricardo first defines rent in the following way:

'*Rent* is that portion of produce of the earth which is paid to the landlord for the use of the original and indestructible powers of the soil.'[5]

He is at pains to point out that the term *rent* is often confused with a combination of rent as he has defined it and profit or the return on capital. In popular language the term is applied to whatever is paid by a farmer to his landlord.[6] He accuses Adam Smith of having used this popular terminology in supposing that payment to a landlord for the privilege of removing [virgin] timber constitutes a payment of rent, whereas in his (Ricardo's) view the payment is for the commodity timber not for the original and indestructible qualities of the soil. Only if a payment were made for the privilege of growing timber could it be termed 'rent'.[7] Ricardo says that the same observation applies to Smith's contention that rent is also paid for coal mines and quarries. In reality the payment is for:

'the value of the coal or stone which can be removed from them, and has no connection with the original and indestructible powers of the land.'[8]

He goes on:

'In the future pages of this work, then, whenever I speak of the *rent of land*, I wish to be understood as speaking of that compensation which is paid to the owner of land for the use of its original and indestructible powers.'[9]

In the next chapter of the *Principles* Ricardo discusses the rent of mines:

'The return for capital from the poorest mine paying no rent would regulate the rent of all the other more productive mines. This mine is supposed to yield the usual profits of stock. All that the other mines produce more than this will necessarily be paid to the owners for rent. Since this principle is precisely the same as that which we have already laid down respecting land it will not be necessary further to enlarge on it.'[10]

Having declared in the previous chapter that payment to the owner of a mine for the privilege of removing its contents is not rent, Ricardo now declares that the rent of mines is explained by precisely the same principle which explains agricultural rent! What can explain this apparent contradiction? In the chapter dealing with the rent of mines Ricardo refers only to the metals. Is it that Ricardo allows the notion of rent to apply to metals and not to stone or coal (or timber for that matter)? Apparently not. In a later chapter, Ricardo discusses Adam Smith's doctrine concerning the rent of land.[11] His purpose is to falsify Smith's proposition that marginal land will afford a rent. In so doing he quotes Smith's analysis of the rent of coal mines at considerable length. He concludes:

'The whole principle of rent is here admirably and perspicuously explained, but every word is as applicable to land as it is to mines...'[12]

Having taken Adam Smith to task in chapter two for speaking of the rent of mines he now applauds his explanation of the principle! A different explanation of this seeming contradiction must be sought.

While rejecting the view that the rent of mines is composed of two parts (rent resulting from differential ease of exploitation of mines and royalty which is payment for the mineral used up) L.C. Gray asserts that this view results from attempts to harmonise the apparent conflict found in Ricardo's *Principles*.[13] But nowhere does Ricardo pursue this bifurcation of the rent of mines himself. However, it can be argued that Ricardo wishes to make a distinction between mines and land which relates to the *basis* for rent. That is, a distinction between the basis of the whole of the rent of mines and the basis for the whole of the rent of land.

In the chapter on rent, Ricardo offers two different terms which may be used to describe the payment for original and indestructible powers. The first of these terms is *rent* which is defined in the opening paragraphs of the chapter before the criticism of

Adam Smith is advanced.[14] The second term offered is *rent of land* which is defined in a similar fashion to *rent* but on the next page - following on from the criticism of Smith.[15] This second definition may be seen as an attempt to provide a more rigorous working definition which distinguishes *rent of land* from *rent of mines* - although no definition of the latter is offered. When discussing mining in the *Principles*, Ricardo sometimes uses the term *rent of mines* when, it might be argued, the dictates of the English language would require only that the term *rent* be used. Also, when comparing the law of rent as it applies to agriculture and to mining Ricardo carefully chooses his words. Speaking of Adam Smith's mistaken view that rent enters into price, Ricardo argues that had Smith understood the principle that the margin pays no rent 'he would have made no distinction between the law which regulates the *rent of mines* and the *rent of land*.'[16] Although Ricardo carefully distinguishes the term *rent of land* from the term *rent of mines*, the italics or other emphasis which might make this distinction clear to all but the most casual reader is absent. Nonetheless, it appears that Ricardo's intention was to introduce some rigour into his argument and, in the light of this definitional rigour, his criticism of Smith's discussion of the rent of mines can be seen as a criticism of Smith's inability to distinguish differences in the *basis* for rent between mining and agriculture: that is, his inability to distinguish *rent of mines* from *rent of land*.[17]

If the above interpretation is correct, then Ricardo must be attributed with the opinion that the rent of mines, while being explained by the same theoretical construct as the rent of land, has a very different basis from that of land. While the exploitation of the former must impair the basis for rent, exploitation of the latter does not.

Ricardo's contradictory treatment of rent in which he first berates Adam Smith for describing payment to the owner of a mine as rent, only to use the term in this context himself at a later stage is satisfactorily reconciled by the above interpretation. Although Ricardo believed that the same theoretical principle governs the payment to a mine owner for use of his mine as governs the payment to a landlord for the use of his farm, the basis for the payment is not the same. The landlord is paid *rent* which is more properly described as *rent of land* while the mine owner receives a payment which, although it is not *rent*, may conveniently be called *rent* or more properly *rent of mines*.[18]

Although a reconciliation of Ricardo's contradiction is made apparent by careful consideration of his text, there remain some unanswered questions. For example, why should Ricardo commence his discussion of rent by defining *rent,* rather than the *rent of land,* as payment for use of the original and indestructible powers of the soil? And why should Smith's unwillingness to recognise the basis of rent of mines as being different from the basis of rent of land be confused with a popular inability to distinguish rent from profit?[19]

Cannan, in his *Theories of Production and Distribution,* also argues that the Ricardian contradiction is one explained by semantics rather than by any problem of contradictory analytical content.[20] His explanation is, however, different from that offered above. Cannan argues that Ricardo, like most people who have not had the advantage of a literary education, was apt to think that a word ought to have whatever sense it was convenient to give it. Thus, although Ricardo was aware that payment to owners of mines was not payment for original and indestructible powers but was payment for the mineral removed, so strong is the power of custom that Ricardo called the payment *rent.*[21] In his later *Review of Economic Theory* Cannan again argues that Ricardo wished to emphasise the fundamental difference between the basis for rent in mining and in agriculture but, contrary to his earlier semantic explanation, argues that the contradiction between the treatment of mines in the chapter on rent and their treatment in the chapter on the rent of mines does have an explanation which relates to the alternative analytical treatment which each may be accorded.[22] Cannan argues that in the chapter on rent, Ricardo was thinking of diminishing returns [on the extensive margin] being the major factor in the creation of agricultural rent but that, at this stage of his exegesis, he considered mines to be different from agriculture since they experienced increasing returns [on the extensive margin] - as evidenced by the historical fall in the prices of the precious metals. Cannan says, however, that when Ricardo turned to his chapter on the rent of mines he was struck by the similarities between mining and agriculture and proceeded on that basis.[23]

If Cannan is correct in asserting that Ricardo abandoned the empirically revealed idea of the mineral industries displaying historically increasing returns in order to have them conform with his theory of agriculture, this interpretation is of great significance in the context of the development of the economic treatment of mineral extraction; for, although Adam Smith and the later

American author Carey both suggested the importance of increasing return on the extensive margin, it was the Ricardian case of diminishing return which was to become an integral part of the economics of exhaustible resources.

By all accounts, including the interpretation offered in this chapter, Ricardo clearly understood the impermanent basis for 'rent' in the mine. This understanding has, of course, been a fundamental aspect of virtually all of the analytical treatments of mineral extraction since Ricardo's time.

Fortunately Ricardo's more general treatment of the mining industries is less contentious - if limited in its scope. Ricardo's concept of the rent of mines being determined by the costs of production at the poorest mine has already been discussed as has the application of this principle in the *Wealth of Nations*. There is, however, a vast difference in the application of this principle between Smith and Ricardo. Whereas Smith also emphasises the role of the intramarginal mine in the determination of price, particularly in a dynamic setting which involves the intrusion of new, intramarginal mines, Ricardo sees the marginal mine as having a preemptive role.

In his early chapter on the rent of mines Ricardo explains that the value of the output of mines is subject to variation. He argued that on the one hand value may fall as a result of improvements in machinery, the discovery of more fertile mines or improvements in transport; on the other, increased value may result from increasing depth of workings or from intrusion of water. Ricardo notes that the more fertile mines of America had a very great effect upon the price of precious metals but argues that, this effect having ceased, any continuing fall in the value of the precious metals must be consequent upon improvements in the mode of working these mines.[24] However, in considering a situation where the demand for coal increases he says:

'If the old mines are insufficient to supply the quantity of coal required, the price of coal will rise, and will continue rising till the owner of a *new and inferior* mine finds that he can obtain the usual profits of stock by working his mine. If his mine be tolerably fertile, the rise will not be great before it becomes his interest so to employ his capital; but if it be not tolerably fertile, it is evident that the price must continue to rise till it will afford him the means of paying his expenses, and obtaining the ordinary profits of stock. It appears, then, that it is always the least fertile mine which regulates the price of coal.'[25]

Having declared that the new mine will be inferior, Ricardo goes on to consider Smith's proposition that the more fertile mine may displace the marginal mine. While acknowledging that displacement of marginal mines may occur, he allows in this case, only that it result from a diminution of demand or by an improved technology which affects all mines:

'If the demand for coal should be diminished or if by new processes the quantity should be increased, the price would fall, and some mines would be abandoned; but in every case, the price must be sufficient to pay the expenses and profits of that mine which is worked without being charged with rent. It is, therefore, the least fertile mine which regulates price.'[26]

In spite of the evidence of the effect of the more fertile American mines, Ricardo emphasises the declining fertility of mines as the extensive margin shifts out. He does so by explaining a process analogous to that used in his treatment of the shift outwards of the extensive margin in agricultural production. Ricardo does acknowledge that the marginal mine may earn a rent, but only because of indivisibilities which prevent the opening of new mines consequent upon a price rise which then affords a rent to the marginal mine. In comparing Smith's approach with Ricardo's it is apparent that Ricardo's emphasis on the role of the marginal mine results from the application of his theory of the rent of land to the mining industry rather than from an independent analysis of the mining industry itself.

Unlike Adam Smith's wide ranging discussion of mines, Ricardo's treatment is mainly confined to an analysis of the determination of the rent of mines; it does not extend to consideration of property relations, risk and its relation to profit or the relationship between value of rents in mining *vis-a-vis* agricultural rents.

Conclusion

There are two lasting legacies of Ricardo's treatment of mines. The first is his identification of the different basis for rent in mining as compared to agriculture. Whereas the original and indestructible qualities which are the basis for rent in agriculture are not impaired by use, the original but destructible qualities which are the basis for 'rent' in mining are. This distinction between mining and agriculture which Ricardo first formally identified was the genesis of the separate branch of economic theory which came to be known generally as the economic theory of exhaustible resources.

The second and more important legacy of Ricardo's treatment of mines is the hypothesis that long run increases in mineral output must come from increasingly inferior mineral deposits. In spite of Adam Smith's optimistic emphasis on the possibility of increasing returns on the extensive margin in mining and in spite of similar views promulgated by later authors, the pessimistic Ricardian emphasis on diminishing returns has by and large been an integral part of the economics of mineral extraction to this day. That is, in spite of suggestions to the effect that user cost in at least some of the mineral industries may be relatively low or even zero, the Ricardian hypothesis involving relatively high user cost has been maintained.

In general, Ricardo's treatment of mines is similar to his analysis of agriculture. Although the basis for rent is different in each case, the static analysis of mines emphasises the unique role for the marginal mine in the determination of price while the dynamic view sees resort to inferior resources over time.

Notes

1. D. Ricardo, *The Principles of Political Economy and Taxation* (Dent, London, 1973), pp. 33-34. The text is that of the 3rd edn, 1821.
2. Ibid., ch. 3.
3. Ibid., ch. 24.
4. Oswald St. Clair in the preface to his *Key to Ricardo* gives a good account of the difficulties various authors have had in understanding Ricardo. O. St. Clair, *Key to Ricardo* (Kelley, New York, 1965). One of the more amusing criticisms of this aspect of Ricardo is offered by H.C. Carey: 'Having studied carefully the works of the most eminent of the recent writers on the subject [of Ricardo's theory] and having found no two of them to agree, [the inquirer] turns, in despair, to Mr. Ricardo himself, and there he finds, in the celebrated chapter on rent, contradictions that cannot be reconciled, and a series of complications such as never before, as we believe, was found in the same number of lines. The more he studies, the more he is puzzled, and the less difficulty does he find in accounting for the variety of doctrines taught by men who profess to belong to the same school, and who all agree, if in little else, in regarding the new theory of rent as

the discovery of the age.' H.C. Carey, *The Past the Present and the Future* (Kelley, New York, 1967), pp. 17-18.

5. Ricardo, *Principles*, p. 33, emphasis added.

6. A brief discussion of the relevance of prevailing institutional arrangements for this distinction between rent and profit can be found in M. Blaug, *Ricardian Economics* (Greenwood Press, Westport, Connecticut, 1958), p. 128.

7. Ricardo, *Principles*, pp. 33-4.

8. Ibid., p. 34.

9. Ibid., emphasis added.

10. Ibid.

11. Ibid., ch. 24.

12. Ibid., p. 221.

13. L.C. Gray, 'Rent under the assumption of exhaustibility', *Quarterly Journal of Economics*, vol. 28 (1914), reprinted in M. Gaffney (ed.), *Extractive Resources and Taxation* (University of Wisconsin Press, Madison, 1967), p. 440. Orchard, although writing after Gray, asserts that Ricardo did indeed consider that mine surplus consists of two parts - rent and royalty. He argues, without supporting evidence, that when Ricardo turned to the question of the nature of the rent of mines and declared it to be determined in the same way as agricultural rent he was assuming that the royalty payment for the mineral removed 'had already been deducted'. J.E. Orchard, 'The rent of mineral lands', *Quarterly Journal of Economics*, vol. 36 (1922), p. 291.

14. Ricardo, *Principles*, p. 33.

15. Ibid., p. 34.

16. Ibid., p. 220, emphasis added.

17. In considering Ricardo's criticism of Smith's position, Marx comes down on the side of Smith. He argues that, properly defined, rent involves 'payment for the *"use"* of natural things, irrespective of whether it is for the use of the "original powers" of the soil or of the power of the waterfall or of land for building or of the treasures to be found in the water or in the bowels of the earth.' Thus payments to owners for the use of agricultural lands, virgin forests or mines are *rent* in every case. K. Marx, *Theories of Surplus Value* (Lawrence and Wishart, London), 1969, pp. 246-7, original emphasis.

18. The idea that Ricardo wished to distinguish different bases for rent is supported by the following quotation from Cassel: 'We have defined rent, in the most general sense of the term, as the price charged for a durable good. It follows that a price paid for consumption goods cannot be rent, not even if those consumption goods are so-called free gifts of nature. Incomes derived from the sale of ore out of a mine or of wood from a primaeval forest are therefore not rents proper, although, practically speaking, their nature is very similar to that of a rent, provided that they are forthcoming over very long periods of time. *Economists have been fully aware of this point ever since Ricardo's time.*' G. Cassel, *The Theory of Social Economy* (Harcourt Brace, New York, 1932), p. 268, emphasis added.

19. Marx considered Ricardo's treatment of mines and forests at length. Although he argued that Ricardo's criticism of Smith for confusing rent with profit involved 'strange logic', he offered no reconciliatory explanation for it. See Marx, *Theories*, pp. 245-6.

20. E. Cannan, *Theories of Production and Distribution* (Staples, London, 1917).

21. Ibid., p. 153.

22. E. Cannan, *A Review of Economic Theory* (Cass, London, 1964).

23. Ibid., pp. 246-8.

24. Ricardo, *Principles*, pp. 46-7.
25. Ibid., p. 222, emphasis added.
26. Ibid. This difference between Smith and Ricardo is further discussed in chapter 6 below.

6

Smith and Ricardo Compared

In the previous chapters dealing with Adam Smith and Ricardo, it has been argued, *inter alia*, that whereas Smith's analysis of the mineral industries emphasised a process in which new, low cost mines intrude into the market, Ricardo considered that resort to new, high cost mines was typical. In discussing these differing views in the chapters above, little consideration was given to the factors which influenced their formation. Were differences in the economic conditions of the mineral industries in Smith's time and in Ricardo's responsible or were there other contributing factors?

This is an important question since the difference between Smith and Ricardo in this respect is a difference between the first two classical authors to consider mining in some detail. It is also the first of a series of similarly conflicting views which were contributed by various authors during the period under review. Indeed, this study has a leitmotif which involves comparison of the differing views which various authors held about the nature of return on the extensive margin in mining - the nature of this return being of primary importance in the determination of the user cost of mineral extraction. The remainder of this chapter involves brief consideration of the question of whether Smith's and Ricardo's conflicting views had an empirical foundation or were the result of some other factor.

The Mineral Industries in Smith's Time and in Ricardo's

There are two particular mining activities to which both Adam Smith and Ricardo refer; namely, precious metal mining in the New World and the domestic coal mining industry - although Adam Smith also refers to a wide range of other mining activities including domestic tin mining and the global mining of precious stones and base metals.

While the decline in price of the precious metals which was associated with the New World discoveries is much emphasised by Smith, it is casually dismissed by Ricardo who sees it as an uncharacteristic, once and for all event. Rather, he prefers to emphasise the role of technology in reducing price by its effect on all mines:

'By the discovery of America, and the rich mines in which it abounds, a very great effect was produced on the natural price of the precious metals. This effect is by many supposed not yet to have terminated. It is probable, however, that all the effects on the value of the metals resulting from the discovery of America have long ceased; and if any fall has of late years taken place in their value, it is to be attributed to improvements in the mode of working the mines.'[1]

Reference has already been made to Cannan's opinion that Ricardo's contradictory treatment of mineral rent resulted from his first wishing to argue, on the basis of the New World discoveries, that minerals are subject to increasing returns on the extensive margin although, ultimately, he was struck by the similarity between mining and agriculture and proceeded to argue that mines, like agricultural lands, are subject to diminishing returns. If Cannan's argument is correct, then it may be justifiably argued that Ricardo's view was, at least in part, a result of his wish to have the mineral industries conform to his existing theory of agricultural rent - thus obviating the need to provide an alternative explanation for the problem of an empirically observed falling cost in the mining of precious metals. Ricardo was able to justify his application of the theory of agricultural rent to mining by relating the chain of events which are to be expected as a result of an increase in demand in the coal mining industry. He argued, as the quotation in the previous chapter shows, that such an event would be associated with development of new and *inferior* mines. While the characteristics of the precious metal mining industries did not suit Ricardo's purpose those of the domestic coal mining industry did. It should also be noted that while for Adam Smith the development of mines in the New World was already history, for Ricardo this development was even more distant in time. Certainly Ricardo may have found it more difficult to dismiss the effect of the South American discoveries had he been writing a century, or even half a century earlier.

Clearly, little inference can be drawn from events associated with the discoveries of the New World, and it is the characteristics of the domestic coal mining industry which must now be considered to see if further light can be thrown on the differences between Smith and Ricardo. Both of these authors must have had opportunities to learn of the characteristics of the coal mining industry at first hand and to have witnessed its role as a driving force in the industrialisation of Great Britain. Smith's analysis of the coal mining industry emphasises a dynamic process in which low cost mines enter the market and ultimately affect the statically determined price. Conversely, Ricardo emphasised the role of the high cost mine in the static determination of price, arguing that the dynamics of entry into the industry involve the opening of new, high cost mines. Fortunately, the question of whether this difference between Smith and Ricardo can be attributed to differences in the coal mining industry which each observed has been addressed by J.U. Nef in his monumental work on the British coal industry.[2]

Nef argues that the difference between Smith and Ricardo may be partly explained by the different conditions which each observed:

'Smith, who was born at Kirkcaldy, probably had under consideration the collieries round the Firth of Forth. In this district, until just before the publication of the *Wealth of Nations*, the demand for coal was expanding much less rapidly than it had expanded in the sixteenth and early seventeenth centuries, or than it was destined to expand at the end of the eighteenth century ... Many new mines were available; the supply of coal on the whole, exceeded the demand; cutthroat competition raged to such an extent that the conditions at the more fertile and better situated mines could at any rate be plausibly represented as tending to settle the selling price... When Ricardo wrote some fifty years later, in the midst of a great boom in the British coal industry, demand over - reached supply, and price much more obviously tended to be regulated by the worst mine worked.'[3]

In this quotation Nef emphasises the different demand conditions existing in the coal mining industry in Smith's time and in

Ricardo's. If Nef's interpretation is taken at face value then it may not be proper to argue (as has been done in the penultimate chapter above) that Smith's treatment of the precious metals is consistent with his discussion of coal mining; for, in the case of the precious metals the significant role for low cost mines comes from changes in supply conditions associated with new discoveries, while, according to Nef, in the coal mining industry the importance of the low cost mine results primarily from a deficiency of demand associated with a decline in the rate of growth in demand.

Although Nef emphasises demand deficiency as the source of Smith's interpretation of the coal mining industry, it can be argued that his description of the industry in Smith's time is not necessarily inconsistent with the dynamic, supply oriented model which has been attributed to Smith here. That is, Nef's description may be interpreted as confirming the idea that new, low cost coal mines intrude into the market altering the industry supply curve in the process. In the quotation above, Nef states that in Smith's time 'many new mines were available.' If, as Nef states, the supply of coal exceeded demand at this time then, presumably, new mines would have been developed only if they were competitive with existing low cost mines. Thus, the oversupply which Nef describes may result, at least in part, from the intrusion of low cost mines into the market. In Smith's time there were many significant economic changes - such as the development of iron making techniques using coke, increasing use of steam power in industry, improvements in transport (canal development in particular) and the movement to the cities - which might have created the conditions under which it was profitable for new, low cost mines to enter the market - altering the ranking of mines and displacing existing high cost mines in the process.[4] Certainly, this interpretation is consistent with Smith's analysis of the dynamic development of agriculture which involves changing relative cost structure between producers located near to the market and those distant from it.

Although Nef's description of the coal industry is consistent with the dynamic process which Smith described, the question still remains as to whether Smith would have emphasised the role of low cost mines had he been writing in Ricardo's time when, as Nef states, there was a great boom in the British coal industry with demand over-reaching supply.

The answer to this question is that, even in Ricardo's time, Smith would probably have emphasised the intrusion of low cost mines, because Smith's methodology was vastly different from Ricardo's. T.W. Hutchison has described Ricardo's departure from Smith's method of integration of *history* with analysis and theory as 'revolutionary'.[5] Thereafter, says Hutchison, economic history was left largely to rebels and outsiders.[6] Hutchison quotes at length Thomas Sowell's explanation of the significance of Ricardo's new methodology:

> 'With Ricardo economics took a major step toward abstract models, rigid and *artificial* definitions, syllogistic reasoning - and the direct application of the results to policy. The historical, the institutional, and the *empirical* faded into the background, and *explicit* social philosophy shrank to a few passing remarks. Comparative statics became the dominant - though usually implicit - approach: Ricardo declared: "I put those immediate and temporary effects quite aside, and fixed my whole attention on the permanent state of things which will result from them."'[7]

Hutchison's assessment of the differences between Smith's and Ricardo's methodologies also suggests that had Ricardo observed at first hand the sort of developments which occurred in the coal mining industry in Smith's time his analysis of the industry would have been no different from that which he presented.

Conclusion

Adam Smith and Ricardo offered distinctly different analyses of the dynamics of the mineral industries. While Smith detected a tendency to historically increasing returns associated with the intrusion of low cost mines, Ricardo asserted the ubiquity of diminishing returns as increasingly inferior mineral resources were brought into production. It is unlikely that the difference in the assessments which each of these authors made can be attributed to the different economic conditions which each observed; rather, it is likely to be attributable to the different methodological approach which each employed. Smith's hypothesis of long run increasing return is the result of his historical cum empirical approach while Ricardo's contrary insistence on the presence of long run diminishing return grew out of the rigour of his abstract method.

Notes

1. D. Ricardo, *The Principles of Political Economy and Taxation* (Dent, London, 1911), p. 47.

2. J.U. Nef, *The Rise of the British Coal Industry* (Cass, London, 1966).

3. Ibid., vol. 1, p. 328 *n*. Nef also refers the reader to J.E.T. Rogers's view that Smith's role for the most fertile mine can only be valid given a situation in which the supply of coal greatly exceeds the demand. See A. Smith, *An Inquiry into the Nature and Causes of the Wealth of Nations*, J.E.T. Rogers (ed.) (Oxford University Press, Oxford, 1869), p. 177 *n*. It is interesting that Nef's description of the coal mining industry which Smith observed suggests that it was similar to the Australian coal mining industry which Mauldon described a century and a half later. See p. 5 above.

4. Improvements in transport may well be the most important of the economic changes which altered the ranking of mines according to cost. Discussing Adam Smith's familiarity with the developments of his time, C.R. Fay remarks that 'his constant emphasis on the cost of bringing a commodity to market puts him closer to us of the 20th century than are his successors, who, dominated by the marvels of factory production, studied too little the economics of marketing and transport.' C.R. Fay, *Great Britain from Adam Smith to the Present Day* (Longmans, Green, London, 1929), p. 4. For a general discussion of improvements in transport in Smith's time see W.T. Jackman, *The Development of Transportation in Modern England* (Cass, London, 1962). Changes in transport as they related to the coal industry are succinctly summarised in B. Lewis, *Coal Mining in the Eighteenth and Nineteenth Centuries* (Longman, London, 1972), ch. 2.

5. T.W. Hutchison, *On Revolutions and Progress in Economic Knowledge* (Cambridge University Press, Cambridge, 1978), p. 54.

6. Ibid., pp. 54-5.

7. Ibid., p. 54 *n*. The emphasis is Hutchison's.

7

Henry Carey

The Maltho-Ricardian theory involving the idea of a growing population pressing up against the capacity of agriculture to feed it and the attendant hypothesis that this state of affairs is associated with the need for increasingly inferior land to be taken into cultivation was roundly criticised by the American economist H.C. Carey. Although Carey's predecessors Young and Chalmers had already pointed out that it was not necessarily the most fertile lands which were first cultivated, it was Carey's opposition to the Maltho-Ricardian idea which in Cannan's words, was the first which made itself heard.[1]

Carey, in his many volumes, devotes an enormous amount of space to refutation of the doctrine - which he most closely associates with Ricardo - that in every country 'the most fertile and most favourably situated land will be first cultivated.'[2] His appeal is to the facts of history which he outlines at great length in his consideration of the historical development of agriculture in most of the North American States and in most of the countries of the world. According to Carey, the natural progression of the development of agricultural land is from high cost to low cost rather than the other way around.[3]

In his consideration of mining, Ricardo argued that in a similar manner to agriculture, increases in mineral output will come from mines which are inferior to those already in operation. Carey makes direct reference to the historical progress of mining and, although Ricardo's position regarding mines is not promulgated, Carey argues that in similar fashion to agriculture, it is often the highest cost mines which are first brought into production. Carey's position regarding the historical development of mines which is in contrast to that of Ricardo will later be seen to be of great

importance in the context of the development of the economic
theory of exhaustible resources; and one of the objectives of this
chapter is to demonstrate that although the order in which
agricultural lands are taken up has little relevance for the static
treatment of agriculture, the order in which mines are exploited
has great significance for the economic theory of exhaustible
resources.

The first section of this chapter deals with Carey's objection to
the Ricardian hypothesis that the natural order of events is for the
most fertile agricultural lands to be cultivated first. This discussion
is then used as a background to the second section of this chapter
which deals with Carey's analysis of the historical progress of the
mineral industries. The third section of this chapter considers
Carey's brief analysis of mineral rent and following this some
critiques of the Carey argument regarding the historical development of agriculture are considered. The chapter concludes with a
summary of the significance of Carey's contribution.

Historical Development in Agriculture

On the basis of his observation of the development of agriculture in the four corners of the earth, Carey argued that rude
societies with little capital (including social overhead capital) had
no choice but to commence cultivation on the poorest soils which
were, at the time, the most accessible. These soils were typically
lightly wooded and situated on high ground. In time, the development of capital stock and growing population brought with them
the capability of unlocking the highly fertile soils of the low lands
which were heavily wooded and difficult of access. This unlocking
of previously inaccessible but fertile soils meant that over time
agricultural output would grow more rapidly than population. The
increasing welfare of mankind is thus seen by Carey to be
guaranteed by the progression from inferior to superior soils; and
this progression is attributable to a range of interrelated factors
including:

a) growth in private capital in the form of superior manufac-
tories, superior agricultural equipment, etc.;

b) growth in social overhead capital such as the creation and
extension of roads and canals; and,

c) the increasing prospects for association, cooperation and
commerce which promote and are promoted by economic
growth.[4]

As may be inferred from the earlier discussion of return in this study, Carey's empirically based hypothesis that it is the least fertile soils which are first cultivated does not imply irrational behaviour on the part of those who first take up agricultural lands. For them, the lands which are first settled are those which, at the time, will produce output at least cost. Over time, however, as capital, technology and population grow, the rank ordering of agricultural lands (in terms of the cost of output they produce) is inverted. Lands having relatively high fertility which, on first settlement, were economically inaccessible have, as a result of the accessibility which accompanies progress, become the low cost farms. On the other hand, lands which have relatively low fertility but which, because of their initial accessibility, once produced output at least cost become the high cost farms. While, at any time, agricultural output will come from both high cost and low cost farms, over time farms which once had high costs will become increasingly intramarginal while farms which once had low costs become increasingly marginal.

Carey's analysis of agriculture involves a dynamic model in which progress and the associated intrusion of new, low cost farms into the market bring with them an increasing abundance of agricultural output. That is, Carey hypothesises increasing returns on the extensive margin in agriculture. Carey's briefer treatment of mines which also invokes the powers of progress in increasing the abundance of mineral output over time is discussed in the next section.

Historical Development in Mining

The major references to mining in Carey's works appear in his *Principles of Political Economy* which was first published in 1837[5] - some 20 years after the publication of Ricardo's *Principles*. There are no references to the economics of mining in *The Past the Present and the Future* (1847)[6] and only scant reference in *The Principles of Social Science* (1858).[7]

As is the case with agriculture, in mining it is the powers of progress which, over time, yield increasingly abundant mineral outputs. On the first settlement of a new land, capital (especially of the social overhead variety) is so scarce that only agricultural and minor commercial activities are worthwhile. In time, however, the growth of infrastructure allows the commencement of manufacturing industry and this development is followed, in turn, by the opening of mines.

Once a mining industry has been established in the new land it will, like agriculture, be subject to historically increasing returns. With progress comes the capacity to mine at greater depths:

'The lower strata of coal are in the situation of the dormant powers of land subjected to cultivation. When coal mines are worked with indifferent machinery, capable of extracting the coal from only a moderate depth, the land is soon worked out, and abandoned. Increased capital enables the miner to descend double the distance, and the value is now greater than at first. A further application of capital enables him to descend successively 300, 500, 600, 1000, or 1500 feet, and with every successive application the property acquires a higher value, notwithstanding the quantity of coal that has been taken out.'[8]

Progress also unlocks mines in previously inaccessible locations, changing, in the process, the rank ordering of lands according to their productivity:

'[A] canal, or a rail road, may be made to this [previously unproductive] land, and the *inferior property, the bed of granite, or of coal, that had been totally unproductive may become worth, perhaps, twenty or fifty times as much as the superior land immediately adjoining it...* We have daily evidence that such is the result of the application of capital. Beds of limestone, that a few years since were comparatively valueless, now yield large revenues. In other places are masses of granite that were unlikely ever to come into use, and of which one hundred acres would have been given for a single acre of land susceptible of cultivation; whereas, a single acre now yields more than one hundred acres of land in its vicinity, of the highest degree of fertility. Thus the different soils change places, and that which was superior becomes inferior, while that which was entirely worthless takes its place at the head of the most productive.'[9]

This process involving increasing returns on the extensive margin is not confined to newly colonised countries such as North America but is apparent in the old countries as well:

'Of the 80 copper-mines of Prussia, no less than 24 have been opened within the last few years. Every mine, every furnace, and every mill, aids in the creation of new roads and the improvement of old ones - facilitating the opening of new mines, the utilization of the powers of nature, and the development of mind; and this increasing the value of man while diminishing that of all the commodities required for his use.'[10]

As well as growth in the capital stock which accompanies, and is accompanied by progress, there are also the forces of association and combination:

'Every furnace that is built, and every mine that is opened, tends to facilitate the further progress in the same direction - because each and every of them tends to promote association and combination.'[11]

Carey's discussion of the historical development of mining indicates two distinct sources of increased productivity. The first of these, which is revealed in the above quotation dealing with the possibility of coal mining at greater and greater depths, involves the application of increased capital and technology in the mine. The increased quantity and quality of capital which facilitates mining of deeper deposits prevent the onset of the historically diminishing returns which might be expected as a result of the progressive exhaustion of the shallower deposits. However, there is more than one way in which this productivity of increased capital and technology may be realised. The increased capital and technology which facilitate the exploitation of deep deposits may, *cet. par.*, just as successfully be directed to increasing the productivity of existing shallow mines.[12] That is, this source of increased productivity does not alter the rank ordering of mines according to their relative cost. *Cet. par.*, existing low cost (shallow) mines will retain their cost advantage over high cost (deep) mines when improved techniques or similar proportional increases in the quantity of capital are applied to each.

The first of Carey's sources of increased productivity in mining is seen to involve the classic case of diminishing returns on the extensive margin being countered by increasing returns to scale and to technology. It is thus not at variance with Ricardo's pessimistic prognosis.

Carey's second source of increased productivity is very different from the first. As a result of the historical development of infrastructure and growing opportunities for association and combination new mines which may be exploited at lower cost than existing mines become available. This process is best exemplified by the quotation above in which Carey discusses the exploitation of previously comparatively valueless coal, limestone and granite deposits. These newly economic mineral deposits are akin to the more fertile agricultural lands of the low country - had they been economically accessible at the time that the older, high cost mines were first developed they would have been exploited then at lower cost than the older, high cost mines. That is, the rank ordering of mineral deposits in terms of relative production cost has been reversed as the forces of progress bring about increasing return on the extensive margin.

Unlike the first source of productivity growth, Carey's second source implies that, even with a given extraction technology and with no increase in the capital intensity of extraction, mineral resources are becoming more abundant over time. Although Carey does not make the point (at least in relation to mining) it also implies that existing mines may suffer obsolescence as a result, not of their impending physical exhaustion, but because they are displaced by new, low cost mines. This possibility of obsolescence involves a similar process to that identified by Adam Smith in his analysis of the world silver market.[13] However, Smith's analysis of the displacement process emphasises random discoveries of superior deposits whereas Carey is speaking of a systematic process in which new, low cost mines become available.[14] The systematic process of progression to superior deposits which Carey has in mind is in stark contrast to Ricardo's insistence that, over time, resort must be had to increasingly inferior resources.

Carey's hypothesis of a natural progression to superior mineral resources is the most significant part of his work in the context of the historical development of the economic theory of exhaustible resources. It will be further discussed in a later part of this chapter and numerous references will be made to it throughout this work. As well as his analysis of historically increasing return in mining, Carey also briefly discusses the rent of mines. This discussion is outlined in the section below.

The Rent of Mines

Carey's discussion of the rent of mines has its purpose in the refutation of Ricardo's argument to the effect that 'rents' paid for the right to remove timber from a [virgin] forest or to remove mineral from a mine are not, in fact, true economic rents since they are not payment for the original and indestructible powers of the soil but are payment for the material removed. Carey's refutation of this argument involves a position which places mining on a par with agriculture. From an economic point of view, Carey sees the difference between mining and agriculture as one of degree rather than of kind.

Using Adam Smith's contentious case of 'rents' paid for forests in Norway, Carey argues that Ricardo is wrong in arguing that these rent payments are not true economic rents.[15] A crop of timber, says Carey, is similar to any other agricultural crop save that it takes longer to reach maturity than many of the more familiar agricultural crops such as onions or wheat. Payments to a landlord for the right to remove mature timber from a particular forest thus occur after a long period of maturation. Nevertheless, these payments are not for the material removed but are by way of compensation for the landlord's expenditure on land taxes and improvements to the property during the maturation period.[16]

Likewise, with mines, there is a long maturation period: 'five, or even ten centuries may be required to prepare to reap the harvest, during the whole of which period, capital has been expending in the preparation therefor.'[17] Thus, says Carey, there is no fundamental difference between mining and small crop farming - each activity yields a rent which is compensation for expenses incurred. But what of Ricardo's emphasis on the indestructible powers of agricultural soil, do these powers not differentiate mines from agricultural land? 'No', replies Carey, for agricultural lands are as easily destroyed as are mineral deposits. If a land owner fails to replenish the fertility of his soil by neglecting the necessary application of manure, labour and capital, his soil will become worthless. In the same way, a mine becomes worthless if its owner neglects to put aside some of the proceeds of its early exploitation so that when the more accessible mineral is exhausted deeper shafts may be sunk. If both agricultural land and mines may be exhausted and if each may be 'replenished' by the appropriate expenditure then there is no fundamental difference between them.[18]

The fundamental and obvious nature of the errors committed by Carey in his analysis of the rent of mines is such as to make a detailed criticism of them superfluous. Suffice it to say that Ricardo's crucial point appears to have escaped Carey entirely; Ricardo's original and indestructible powers are just that (as his criticism of those unable to differentiate between rent and profit makes clear); and rent is paid for these powers, not as compensation for expenditure by the landlord.

Although Carey's analysis of the rent of forests and of mines displays the ingenuity of a contortionist, it is the convincing nature of his arguments for the presence of increasing returns on the extensive margin in agriculture which gave him prominence in the literature of economics. Many of the authors whose work is reviewed in later chapters make reference to Carey's case for historically increasing returns in agriculture. Their assessments of that case are considered later along with their contributions to the development of the economic theory of exhaustible resources. However, there are many other authors who have passed judgment and the opinions of some of them are considered in the next section.

Critiques of the Hypothesis of Increasing Return

The general tenor of critiques of Carey's hypothesis is to the effect that the argument for increasing returns on the extensive margin in agriculture is basically correct but that the correctness of the argument does not detract from Ricardo's theory of rent - it detracts only from the pessimistic prognosis of the Maltho-Ricardian doctrine. Cannan assesses the validity of Carey's hypothesis in the following terms: '[Carey] went too far in his belief in the advantages of a large and growing population, but he was right in denying flatly that the returns to agricultural industry have diminished in the past.'[19]

Describing Carey's optimistic vision as being 'independent of its deplorable analytic implementation and capable of being implemented more satisfactorily', Schumpeter calls it a 'great' vision which expressed adequately both the situation and the spirit of the United States.[20] Schumpeter goes on to say that although a case may be put for Carey's hypothesis of increasing return on the extensive margin, the hypothesis is not, as Carey believed, relevant to the Ricardian theory.[21]

The irrelevance of Carey's hypothesis for the Ricardian theory is well paraphrased by Pantaleoni - although he does not specifically mention Carey:

'It must be borne in mind, that the fertility of land can only be discussed *with reference to some particular kind of produce*, a point Ricardo emphasised by considering it with reference to only *one kind*, viz. wheat. This being so, Ricardo's theory is not disproved by demonstrating inductively, that with the progress of civilization and the consequent changes in human wants, sandy soils have come to be more valued than heavy soils, or *vice versa*. It must further be borne in mind, that the fertility of any soil is always relative to the means available for cultivating it; or in other words, that the maximum fertility consists in the maximum difference between production and cost. Hence Ricardo's theory is not refuted by proving inductively that lighter and less fertile soils were cultivated first, and that the cultivation of richer soils was undertaken only when the technical arts were more advanced, and capital and labour more abundant. Indeed that argument confirms his theory, inasmuch as it proves that the lighter soils were cultivated before the others, because the costs involved in tilling them was so much less than would have been required, at that time, to cultivate the richer soils: that the net produce of the former was more than that of the latter.'[22]

Finally, mention should be made of the reconciliatory interpretation of the Ricardo - Carey dispute which was suggested by af Heurlin and which was later reviewed by Ralph Turvey in the *Economic Journal*.[23] Turvey explains that if the short run marginal cost curves of (say) two farms intersect, then at low levels of output one of the farms will have least cost while at higher levels of output the other will have the least cost. Thus, as output rises over time the ranking of land according to its production cost is inverted. Herr af Heurlin described this result as 'the law of changing order of rent.'[24] Turvey concludes that the dispute between Ricardo and Carey can be reconciled entirely within the realm of theory: Ricardo is correct if the marginal cost curves do not intersect (that is, if one farm has its marginal cost curve wholly above that of the other) while Carey is right if the marginal cost curves do intersect. Whether this explanation does in fact reconcile the dispute between Carey and Ricardo is a moot point; af Heurlin's explanation of the inversion process is strictly short run and, although changes which occur over historical time may be relevant in the short run, Carey's criticism of Ricardo's statement of the tendency to diminishing return on the extensive margin emphasises historical changes in factors such as technology, the size of the capital stock and industrial organization which are long run factors.

The opinions regarding Carey which are offered by some of the authors considered in later chapters serve to reinforce the assessment of those authors who are quoted above; namely, that no matter what the order of fertility in which agricultural lands are taken up, all that is required for the Ricardian theory of rent to hold is that there are lands of differing degrees of fertility being worked at any time.

Conclusion

The significance of Carey's contribution to the economic theory of exhaustible resources lies in his optimistic suggestion that mining - like agriculture - may be characterised by increasing return on the extensive margin. However, Carey gave no indication that he was aware that his hypothesis of increasing return on the extensive margin in mining might have particular relevance for production decisions in the individual mine.

J.S. Mill whose contribution is considered shortly, clearly identifies the possibility that antagonism between present and future production will characterise extraction from the mine; and this is a theme which recurs throughout the later mineral economics literature. Now, Carey's first source of historically increasing return which involves the potential for lowering of costs for *all* mines as the result of the application of increased capital and technology does nothing to counter the problem of the need to resort to inferior deposits as exhaustion of currently worked deposits occurs. As was indicated in the earlier chapter dealing with return, resort to inferior resources implies that extraction from mines which are currently being worked involves user cost. In this case the owner of a mine which is currently being worked will find that as society resorts to increasingly inferior deposits over time, his finite deposit is likely to become more valuable over time; and this rising value means that user cost of present production is likely to be relatively high. On the other hand, user cost will be relatively low or even zero in Carey's second case of historically increasing returns which involves increasing return on the extensive margin associated with the development of new mines having lower production cost than existing mines. As the rank order of deposits is altered by the intrusion of new, low cost mines, the owner of an existing mine finds that its value (if it has one) declines as it becomes increasingly marginal over time.

As the contemporary theory of exhaustible resources indicates, the extent of user cost is an important determinant of production decisions in the mine. Thus decisions made by mine owners operating in an environment characterised by Carey's first case of historically increasing return will, because of the significantly greater user cost involved, be different from those made by owners operating in an environment typified by his second case.

There is clearly no evidence that Carey was aware of any significant difference in the implications for mining of the two sources of historically increasing return which he identified. Indeed, in the case of agriculture which is the major activity examined by Carey, there is no such difference. If it is assumed that predatory farming is not practiced, the presence of an environment such as is suggested by Carey's second case (progression to superior resources) will not, as the quotation above from Professor Pantaleoni shows, alter the statically determined profit maximising level of output as compared to an environment characterised by the first case in which, *cet. par.*, a Ricardian resort to inferior resources occurs.[25] Production decisions in each case are not different since, in each case, there is no difference in user cost - if there is user cost at all.

Although Carey's second case involving progression to superior resources can be shown to be of considerable significance for the economic theory of exhaustible resources, this significance was presumably not understood by Carey and was certainly not made explicit by him, nor, as the following chapters will show, was it indicated by later authors who also considered the possibility of increasing return on the extensive margin. On the other hand, while Carey might have considered his negation of Ricardo's distinction between mining and agriculture to have been of some lasting significance, it is seen, in terms of the development of the economic theory of mineral extraction, to represent a retrograde step.

Notes

1. E. Cannan, *Theories of Production and Distribution* (Staples, London, 1917), p. 137.

2. These are Ricardo's words. D. Ricardo, *The Principles of Political Economy and Taxation* (Dent, London, 1911), p. 37.

3. In this context, 'cost' is taken to mean the costs of bringing output to market and includes production cost, transport cost, etc.

4. The way in which these three factors promote historically increasing return is described by Carey in numerous places throughout his works; indeed there is hardly a page in which at least one of them is not discussed or alluded to. Carey's major works are: *Principles of Political Economy* (1837), *The Past the Present and the Future* (1847) and *Principles of Social Science* (1858).

5. H.C. Carey, *Principles of Political Economy* (Kelley, New York, 1967).

6. H.C. Carey, *The Past the Present and the Future* (Kelley, New York, 1967).

7. H.C. Carey, *Principles of Social Science* (Kelley, New York, 1963).

8. Ibid., p. 41.

9. Ibid., pp. 134-5, original emphasis.

10. Carey, *Principles of Social Science*, vol. 2, p. 133.

11. Ibid.

12. Carey makes this point explicitly. Carey, *Principles of Political Economy*, vol. 1, pp. 240-1.

13. See p. 58 above.

14. Adam Smith may have had a similar systematic process in mind when he considered the domestic coal mining industry. See p. 56-7 above.

15. See p. 67 above.

16. Carey, *Principles of Political Economy*, vol. 1, p. 188. Carey appears to be speaking of virgin forests although he does not make this clear.

17. Ibid., p. 189.

18. This view of mines is similar to Adelman's contemporary perception of the oil industry. See p. 31n13 above.

19. Cannan, *Theories*, p. 137.

20. J.A. Schumpeter, *History of Economic Analysis* (George, Allen and Unwin, London), 1954, pp. 516-7, original emphasis.

21. Ibid., p. 518 n.

22. M. Pantaleoni, *Pure Economics* (Macmillan, London, 1898), p. 277-8, original emphasis.

23. R. Turvey, 'A Finnish contribution to rent theory', *Economic Journal*, vol. 65 (1955), pp. 346-8.

24. Ibid., p. 348. Alfred Marshall had earlier drawn a similar conclusion but had done so in a less formal way: 'There is no absolute measure of the richness or fertility of land. Even if there be no change in the arts of production, a mere increase in the demand for produce may invert the order in which two adjacent pieces of land rank as regards fertility. The one which gives the smaller produce, when both are uncultivated, or when the cultivation of both is equally slight, may rise above the other and justly rank as the more fertile when both are cultivated with equal thoroughness.' A. Marshall, *Principles of Economics*, 8th edn, 1949 resetting (Macmillan, London, 1920), p. 131.

25. However, predatory farming may be optimal on lands which are currently marginal but are soon to become submarginal.

8
J.S. Mill

J.S. Mill's fundamental contributions to economic and philosophical thought are of such significance that although many authors have assessed his work, consideration of relatively less important matters such as his treatment of mining have been largely ignored.[1] Nonetheless, Mill's treatment of mining can be shown to involve a position which emphasises the fundamentally different economic nature of mining as compared to agriculture and which uses this difference as the basis for significant further development of the work of his predecessors.

This chapter comprises two parts. The first and major part discusses Mill's treatment of mining; the second and minor part gives brief consideration to Mill's assessment of Carey's argument for increasing return on the extensive margin in agriculture. The chapter closes with some concluding remarks which suggest that two different models of the nature of the mineral industries can be distilled from Mill's work.

The Treatment of Mining

Mill's numerous references to the mining industries are scattered here and there throughout his *Principles of Political Economy*.[2] This dispersion of material relating to mines results, *inter alia*, from his methodological approach which involves initial consideration of general principles as they apply to agricultural land after which the question of the relevance of these principles for minerals and other natural agents is considered.

Mill's first reference to mines in the *Principles* is thus found in the introductory chapter dealing with the requisites of production where it follows his discussion of the relative abundance of agricultural land. An indication to the reader of the importance of the relative abundance of natural agents is one of the major objectives of this introductory chapter and Mill indicates this importance by considering natural agents to fall into either one or the other of two categories of abundance. In the first category are agents which are effectively unlimited in quantity and have no value in the market; in the second are those which, by virtue of their limited quantity, acquire an exchangeable value. Minerals may fall into either of these two categories:

> 'Coal, metallic ores, and other useful substances found in the earth, are still more limited than [agricultural] land. They are not only strictly local, but exhaustible; although at a given place and time, they may exist in much greater abundance than would be applied to present use even if they could be obtained gratis.'[3]

Although it is not clear whether the minerals which Mill identifies as being in greater abundance than would be demanded at zero price are minerals which exist in deposits that are currently being mined (such as quarry material) or those which exist in large quantities only below the margin of current production, he does make it clear that minerals are location specific and are exhaustible.

It is this exhaustibility of minerals which Mill uses as the basis for his discussion of their susceptibility to the 'law of diminishing returns'. Although in discussing diminishing returns in agriculture, Mill distinguishes decreasing return on the extensive margin (recourse to inferior land) from the law of variable proportions (more intensive exploitation of currently used lands), when turning to the relevance of diminishing return in mining he does not, at this stage, consider the latter aspect of return. He does, however, consider the nature of return on the extensive margin at length as well as commenting on the likelihood of diminishing returns to cumulative extraction.

Mill argues that the presence of diminishing returns to cumulative extraction in mining distinguishes it from agriculture and is responsible for an historical tendency to diminishing return in mining which is more marked than in agriculture. On the other hand, he notes that the opportunities for the operation of antagonistic forces which lead to increasing returns are also more marked in mining:

'As a mine does not reproduce the coal or the ore taken from it, not only are all mines at last exhausted, but even when they as yet show no signs of exhaustion, they must be worked at an ever increasing cost; shafts must be sunk deeper, galleries driven farther, greater power applied to keep them clear of water; the produce must be lifted from a greater depth, or conveyed a greater distance. The law of diminishing return applies therefore to mining, in a still more unqualified sense than to agriculture: but the antagonizing agency, that of improvements in production, also applies in a still greater degree. Mining operations are more susceptible of mechanical improvements than agricultural; the first great application of the steam-engine was to mining; and there are unlimited possibilities of improvement in the chemical processes by which the metals are extracted. There is another contingency, of no unfrequent occurrence, which avails to counter balance the progress of all existing mines towards exhaustion: this is, the discovery of new ones, equal or superior in richness.' [4]

Although Mill's discussion of the importance for diminishing return of cumulative extraction is novel in the context of the economic literature dealing with mineral extraction, it is his optimistic treatment of the long term prospects for mining which is of more interest.[5] His consideration of this aspect is seen in the above quotation to be evocative of both Carey's and Adam Smith's earlier treatments.[6] Certainly, it is at variance with Ricardo's insistence on recourse to inferior deposits over time.

At a later stage in the *Principles*, Mill returns to the question of the nature of the dynamics of mining. However, this time he considers fisheries as well as mines by lumping the two together. As he had already done for mines alone, he argues that, over time, new mines or fisheries of superior quality to those already in use are liable to be opened. His discussion of these dynamics again has much in common with Adam Smith's and with Carey's earlier treatments of the dynamics of mining. It optimistically suggests a progression to superior resources which contrasts, as was noted earlier, with Ricardo's pessimistic emphasis on recourse to inferior resources. It is worth quoting Mill's explanation of the dynamics of mines and fisheries in full:

'Both in the case of mines and of fisheries, the natural order of events is liable to be interrupted by the opening of a new mine, or a new fishery, of superior quality to some of those already in use. The first effect of such an incident is an increase of the supply; which of course lowers the value, to call forth an increased demand. This reduced value may be no longer sufficient to remunerate the worst of the existing mines or fisheries, and these may consequently be *abandoned*. If the superior mines or fisheries, with the addition of the one newly opened produce as much of the commodity as is required at the lower value corresponding to their lower cost of production the fall of value will be permanent, and there will be a corresponding fall in the rents of those mines or fisheries which are not abandoned. In this case, when things have permanently adjusted themselves, the result will be, that the scale of qualities which supply the market will have been cut short at the lower end, while a new insertion will have been made in the scale at some point higher up: and the worst mine or fishery in use - the one which regulates the rents of the superior qualities and the value of the commodity - will be a mine or fishery of better quality than that by which they were previously regulated.'[7]

Like Adam Smith, Mill introduces the idea of mines being abandoned - that is being relinquished as a consequence of falling output prices before physical exhaustion occurs. Occurrences such as this are like those of which Carey spoke in explaining what has been here called his second case of historically increasing return; the case which involves increasing return on the extensive margin and which is characterised by the intrusion of new, low cost mines. Indeed, in the above quotation Mill makes specific reference, as Carey had done, to changes in the ranking of mineral deposits (and fisheries) which give increasing return on the extensive margin.

It was earlier remarked that Mill's initial discussion of diminishing return in mining is devoid of any consideration of short run diminishing return. The reasons for this omission are made clear when he later addresses the matter as part of his consideration of the rent of mines in his chapter on rent in its relation to value. He there argues that the existence of a number of operating mines in an industry may not necessarily be evidence of the existence of short run diminishing returns. Although, in some mines, the limited surface of mineral exposed means that there is a limitation to the number of labourers who may be simultaneously employed, this limitation does not apply to all mines:

'In collieries, for example, some other cause of limitation must be sought for. *In some instances the owners limit the quantity raised in order not too rapidly to exhaust the mine*; in others there are said to be combinations of owners, to keep up a monopoly price by limiting the production.' [8]

In satisfying his need to explain why a number of mines operate at the same time although short run diminishing returns do not apply, Mill has, in the emphasised part of his explanation quoted above, discussed for the first time in the literature the idea of a fundamental difference between decision making in the mine and on the farm. This fundamental difference involves the idea that unlike agriculture, mining may be characterised by an antagonism between present and future production which requires an optimal time profile of production. [9] Regardless of the reasons for its having been made, this observation is, in the context of the development of the theoretical treatment of the economics of exhaustible resources, of immense significance. The idea that the exhaustibility of a finite mineral deposit means that present and future production are antagonistic and that the mine owner-operator must therefore consider the appropriate time profile of production has become a basic feature of the neoclassical treatment of mineral extraction.

Mill's discussion of return in mining is followed by a static analysis of the rent of mines which is unremarkable and which represents no advance from Ricardo's earlier treatment. Price, he says will be regulated by costs in the least fertile mine and all other mines will earn a rent, the value of which is determined by their superiority over the marginal mine. [10] If indivisibilities exist the marginal mine may, as Ricardo had already indicated, also earn a rent; however, the idea that the marginal mine may yield a surplus when no indivisibilities exist is not canvassed here, although Mill gives it prominence at a later stage.

It is clear that Mill sees two possibilities for the historical progress of mining. On the one hand, he writes in Ricardian fashion of a natural order of events involving recourse to inferior resources over time while, on the other, he argues that this natural order of events is 'liable to be interrupted' by the opening of new, low cost mines. Mill's idea that colliery owners will restrict output to extend the life of the mine is consistent with the Ricardian natural order; while his assertion that this natural order is liable to be interrupted by the opening of new, superior mines is consistent with the alternative views of Adam Smith and Carey.[11]

Mill's final significant reference to mines in the *Principles* appears in his concluding remarks to the chapter on rent in relation to value. One of Mill's objectives in discussing rent in relation to value is to reassert the invalidity of the idea held by some of his predecessors - including Adam Smith - that all agricultural land, including marginal land, yields a rent.[12] However, in asserting that there can, in reality, be no rent on the margin of production, he does allow the theoretical possibility of such an outcome - at least in the case of mines:

'A commodity may, no doubt, in some contingencies yield a rent even under the most disadvantageous circumstances of its production; but only when it is, for the time, in the condition of those commodities which are absolutely limited in supply, and it is therefore selling at a scarcity value; which never is, nor has been, nor can be, a permanent condition of any of the great rent-yielding commodities: unless through their approaching exhaustion, if they are mineral products, (coal, for example,) or through an increase of population, continuing after a further increase of production becomes impossible; a contingency, which the almost inevitable progress of human culture and improvement in the long interval which has first to elapse, forbids us to consider as probable.'[13]

That Mill considers the existence of rent on the margin to be more a theoretical possibility than an actual state of affairs is evidenced by the following quotation which comes from his next chapter dealing with the theory of value:

'Rent is not an element in the cost of production of the commodity which yields it: except in the cases (rather conceivable than actually existing) in which it results from, and represents, a scarcity value.'[14]

Regardless of whether it is practically or theoretically possible, Mill's idea that the marginal mine may, under certain circumstances, normally yield a surplus is a novel one which is of great significance in the context of the development of the economics of exhaustible resources. As the following chapters will show, this idea was to become a commonplace, if sometimes contentious, feature of the literature. Before turning to the appraisal of Carey's arguments for increasing return on the extensive margin which Mill offered, some brief conclusions regarding his analysis of mining will be drawn.

Mill's original contribution to the economic theory of mineral extraction involves two closely related ideas. The first of these is the idea that present and future production from the mine may be antagonistic; the second, that theoretically, at least, the marginal mine may normally yield a rent. Now, both of these ideas which, by their very nature, rely on a pessimistic Ricardian prognosis were advanced by later authors. However, the alternative view of mining which Mill offers and which validates Smith's and Carey's idea of increasing return on the extensive margin in the case of at least some mineral industries was not sufficient to save this view from relative obscurity. Mill's consideration of Carey's case for increasing return on the extensive margin in agriculture is briefly considered in the next section.

Increasing Return on the Extensive Margin

Describing Carey as 'an American political economist of merit', Mill uses an extensive footnote to discuss Carey's idea that Ricardo's rent theory is rendered invalid by the observed historical progression to superior agricultural lands.[15] Mill argues that in considering a new country, Carey's hypothesis is frequently correct but that even if it were true of old countries this would have no significance for the Ricardian rent theory - all that is required for that theory to hold true is that there exists at any time, land having differing degrees of fertility.

Although Mill makes no reference to Carey's treatment of mining, it is clear that his own suggestion of the possibility of increasing returns on the extensive margin in mining closely parallels Carey's treatment of both mining and agriculture. However, unlike Carey, Mill also gives prominence to the Ricardian case of diminishing return on the extensive margin in mining.

Conclusion

J.S. Mill's treatment of mines suggests two possible scenarios for a mineral industry. Firstly, the natural order of events is such that over time recourse must be had to increasingly inferior resources - and, if the natural order prevails, then mine owners may find it profitable to limit production from the mine in order to pursue the appropriate time profile of production. That such a limitation is the result of exhaustibility rather than the effect of short run diminishing returns is made clear by Mill when he argues that some mines may be free from the strictures of short run diminishing returns. A further implication of the natural order is that at some time in the future - if not in the present - the impending exhaustion of a mineral may give rise to scarcity rents such that the value of mineral output is greater than extraction cost in the marginal mine.

Both of the implications of the natural order which Mill introduced are novel and are a logical extension of Ricardo's treatment of mines which emphasised exhaustibility and diminishing returns on the extensive margin. They represent the next stage in the development of the economic theory of exhaustible resources following on from Ricardo's work and are found today either explicitly or implicitly in the body of modern economic theory dealing with the subject.

Mill's second scenario for a mineral industry involves an interruption to the natural order of events in which discovery of deposits equal or superior to those in production reduces output price with the result that some existing mines are abandoned. In putting forward this scenario Mill introduces no novel aspects. Although he does not acknowledge Adam Smith or Carey in this context, his treatment of increasing return on the extensive margin clearly echoes their earlier work. In spite of the authority of the classical authors who promoted this viewpoint, it is one which is seldom addressed today in the literature. It was, however, taken up by Marx whose contribution is considered in the next chapter.

In short, Mill suggests two possible models of a mineral industry. In the first, diminishing returns on the extensive margin prevail and user cost is likely to be relatively high; in the second, increasing returns are experienced on the extensive margin and user cost is likely to be relatively low or even zero.

Notes

1. Barnett and Morse do quote some parts of Mill's treatment of mining in discussing his general position on the question of natural resource scarcity. H.J. Barnett and C. Morse, *Scarcity and Growth* (Johns Hopkins Press, Baltimore, for Resources for the Future, 1963), pp. 64-71.

2. J.S. Mill, *Principles of Political Economy* (Routledge, London, 1895). The text is that of the second edition (1840). Mill's references to mining are almost identical in each of his seven editions of the *Principles*.

3. Mill, *Principles*, p. 30.

4. Ibid., p. 136.

5. In his review of the modern theory of optimal depletion of the mine, A.C. Fisher acknowledges Mill as the source of the idea of diminishing returns to cumulative extraction. A.C. Fisher, *Resource and environmental economics* (Cambridge University Press, Cambridge, 1981), p. 24.

6. In his introduction to Mill's *Principles*, V.W. Bladen argues that although Mill had been raised in the Ricardian tradition, his *Principles* was more in the tradition of Adam Smith. V.W. Bladen and J.M. Robson (eds), *Collected Works of John Stuart Mill* (University of Toronto Press, Toronto, 1965), vol. 2, p. xxvii.

7. Mill, *Principles*, pp. 324-5, emphasis added.

8. Ibid., p. 324, emphasis added.

9. Insofar as the farmer has the choice of harvesting his crop 'early' or 'late' there will, of course, be a similarity between agriculture and mining.

10. Mill, *Principles*, p. 324.

11. In discussing the characteristics of the stationary state at a later stage in the *Principles*, Mill reasserts the relevance of the natural order when he argues that the only products of industry which would display increases in production cost in the stationary state are those which rely on non-renewable, exhaustible materials such as minerals. Mill, *Principles*, p. 465.

12. Ibid., pp. 322-3.

13. Ibid., p. 326. Mill was a supporter of Jevons's pessimistic position on the question of the future availability of coal in the United Kingdom and his reference to impending exhaustion of coal in this quotation is consistent with that support. See L.H. Courtney, 'Jevons's Coal Question: thirty years after', *Royal Statistical Society Journal*, vol. 15., no. 4 (1897), p. 789.

14. Mill, *Principles*, p. 327.

15. Ibid., p. 294 *n*. This extensive footnote first appears in the second edition (1849) and, with minor changes, was included in the third, fourth and fifth editions after which it was omitted.

9

Karl Marx

The following discussion of Marx's treatment of mineral extraction involves no attempt to evaluate Marxian economic theory in general. As was explained in the introductory chapter, the contributions of the authors who are reviewed here are being evaluated from the standpoint of contemporary price theory. Thus, although a comprehensive descriptive account of Marx's treatment of mineral extraction will be offered in this chapter, critical assessment of this treatment will be undertaken only in the context of its relevance for the development of the mainstream literature of the economics of exhaustible resources.

Marx undertakes a thorough discussion of mineral extraction in two of his numerous published works. In volume three of *Capital* which was first published in 1885 there is some discussion of mine rent and of what Marx calls the 'extractive' industries.[1] However, a more extensive discussion of mines occurs in his reviews of the work of Adam Smith and Ricardo which appear in *Theories of Surplus Value*. Although Marx's collaborator Engels intended publishing this work as volume four of *Capital*, his death meant that it was left to Karl Kautsky to undertake this task and the work which is now described as *Theories of Surplus Value* was not published until the first decade of this century - and then only in German. The first English translation of this work was published in 1951.[2] However, it did not contain those parts in which Marx discussed at length Ricardo's and Smith's treatment of mines. Not until the Progress Press version was published in the United Kingdom in 1968 was this discussion made available in English.[3]

In the introduction to this study it was made clear that its concern was with the literature of the economics of mineral extraction which was either first published in English or translated into English within the period under review. On the basis of this criterion, Marx's *Theories of Surplus Value* does not qualify for assessment and it is only his treatment of mining in volume three of *Capital* which will be reviewed here. However, this limitation does not preclude the use of relevant aspects of *Theories of Surplus Value* as an aid to understanding the treatment of mineral extraction in *Capital*. Indeed, Marx's discussions of Smith and Ricardo in *Theories of Surplus Value* have already been referred to in the chapters dealing with these authors.

This chapter comprises two main sections. In the first section Marx's treatment of mineral extraction in *Capital* is described and evaluated; in the second, his position regarding Carey's argument for increasing return on the extensive margin is considered. Finally, some concluding remarks are made.

The Treatment of Mineral Extraction

Of the classical economists, it is likely that Marx had the most to say about mining. However, his emphasis was upon the conditions of labour in the mine - in English coal mines in particular - and in *Capital* only scant reference is made to the principles of the economics of mining and to the rent of mines. In *Capital* there are two separate discussions of natural resource based industries which deal with mineral extraction. These discussions deal with mining proper and with what Marx describes as the 'extractive' industries.

As the following quotation from volume one of *Capital* indicates, Marx was aware of the potential for exhaustion of the soil:

> 'all progress in capitalistic agriculture is a progress in the art, not only of robbing of the labourer, but of robbing the soil; all progress in increasing the fertility of the soil for a given time is a progress towards ruining the lasting sources of that fertility. The more a country starts its development on the foundation of modern industry, like the United States, for example, the more rapid is this process of destruction. Capitalist production, therefore, develops technology, and the combining together of various processes into a social whole, only by sapping the original sources of all wealth - the soil and the labourer.'[4]

On the other hand, in his treatment of the rent of mines in chapter 46 of volume three of *Capital*, Marx makes no specific reference to exhaustibility.[5] Although the title of this chapter indicates that it is concerned with mining rent, in this chapter Marx, in a manner reminiscent of Ricardo's treatment of the rent of mines, states only that mining rent proper is 'determined in the same way as agricultural rent.'[6] He goes on to quote, verbatim, the passage from the *Wealth of Nations* in which Smith discusses mines which yield no rent, can thus only be worked by the landlord and which are exemplified by many of the coal mines of Scotland.[7] However, he gives no explanation as to why this passage is quoted.[8] Nowhere in this chapter does Marx aver to exhaustibility as a feature of mines; indeed, he characteristically counters his previous observation regarding the exhaustibility of the soil by concluding the chapter with the observation that the soil, if properly treated, improves all the time and is, unlike fixed capital, able to benefit from successive investments of capital without loss of previous investments.[9]

Although Marx's treatment of the rent of mines in chapter 46 of *Capital* is cursory, he does, in the previous chapter, make reference to industries such as forestry, fishing and quarrying which he describes as 'extractive' industries. In this context, Marx makes no distinction between minerals and other natural resources. Thus fisheries and virgin forests are treated in the same way as are quarries.

Marx argues that the extractive industries are characterised by an absence of capital in the form of raw material and thus have the lowest organic composition of capital of any industries (are highly labour intensive). Since living labour is the only source of surplus value, in these industries more surplus labour is set in motion than in industries where the organic composition of capital is higher (those which are more capital intensive).[10] For this reason there is the potential for surpluses in these industries to be relatively high. The potential exists for capitalists in these industries to derive a more than average profit on their relatively small capital while there is also the potential for a considerable rent surplus to accrue to the owner of the resource. But, says Marx, owing to the ease with which the extractive industries can be expanded these potential surpluses are not realised and the output of the extractive industries is typically sold at prices which are less than exchange values. Thus the entire surplus of unpaid labour (net of the capitalist's profit) does not accrue to the owner of the resource (the landlord) in the form of rent.[11]

In other words, since the supply of *in situ* resources in these industries is highly elastic, competition between owners results in their receiving rents which do not reflect the whole of the surplus labour time expended in the industry. It is Adam Smith's case of the virgin forests of Norway which Marx uses to illustrate his point:

> 'owing to the ease with which timber felling may be extended, in other words, its production rapidly increased, the demand must rise very considerably for the price of timber to equal its value, and thereby for the entire surplus of unpaid labour (over and above that portion which falls to the capitalist as average profit) to accrue to the owner in the form of rent.'[12]

Marx's conclusions about the extractive industries hinge upon two basic features of these industries; namely, that the organic composition of capital is low and that the supply of *in situ* resources is relatively elastic. It is unclear, however, just which of the mineral industries Marx includes in the category of 'extractive' industries. Although he cites quarrying as belonging to this class, as noted above he accords separate treatment to mines in *Capital*. He concludes that the requirement for large amounts of machinery and other fixed capital in mines gives them a higher organic composition of capital than is typical in the extractive industries. This conclusion is, however, inconsistent with his discussion of Ricardo's theory of rent in *Theories of Surplus Value*. He there includes coal mines in the class of industry which has a low organic composition of capital.[13]

Whether or not there are other mining activities which come into Marx's category of extractive industries is a question which must remain unanswered. However, it is clear that the criteria by which resources may be judged to qualify for the extractive class do not involve the idea of antagonism between present and future production. Similarly, this idea is not suggested in the case of those mining activities which do not come into the extractive class. Marx's unwillingness to use the inevitability of natural resource depletion in mining and quarrying as the basis for a fundamentally different analysis of these industries as compared to agriculture is consistent with his declaration that mineral rent is similar to, and is determined in the same way as, agricultural rent.

With this background to Marx's analysis of mining and quarrying some conclusions may be drawn about the overall significance of his treatment of these activities.

Conclusions Regarding Mining and Quarrying

While Marx does distinguish between mining and the extractive industries which include quarrying, it is clear that this distinction in no way relates to whether there is any antagonism between present and future production. It relates only to the organic composition of capital which, he says, is relatively low in the extractive industries and relatively high in mining. There is thus no reason why some quarrying activities having a high organic composition of capital should not be included in the general category of 'mining' while some mining activities having a low organic composition of capital should not be thought of as belonging to the 'extractive' industries - along with fishing and forestry. Certainly, no distinction should be made between any of the natural resource based industries on the basis of the nature of the surplus which accrues to the owner of the resource. Income which accrues by virtue of ownership to the owner of the mine, quarry, forest or farm is rent in every case.

Since Marx distinguishes between different natural resource based industries, including mining, only on the basis of the organic composition of capital relevant to each and since he declares mineral rent to be the same as agricultural rent, it must be concluded that in terms of the development of the mainstream literature of the economics of mineral extraction, Marx's treatment of mining in *Capital* represents no advance from the work of his bourgeois predecessors. Indeed, in terms of bourgeois criteria, his analysis of mines may be seen to be inferior to that of Ricardo and Mill who both emphasised the relevance for mining of the impermanent nature of the key natural resource involved. Although Marx makes no advance in relation to the development of the mainstream literature of the economics of mineral extraction, the question may still be asked as to whether any significant inference can be drawn from his treatment of mines and of the extractive industries.

According to Marx, a basic feature of the extractive industries is low rents which result from the ease with which output may be expanded. In *Capital*, Marx argues that quarries have this characteristic (and later, in *Theories of Surplus Value* he makes the same point in relation to coal mines). It is interesting that this conclusion is similar to Adam Smith's finding that the rent of mines has a small share in the price of their output.[14]

This idea that output may be readily expanded in the extractive industries is, of course, consistent with the idea that there is, in these industries, no marked tendency to decreasing return on the extensive margin.[15] It is thus consistent with the optimistic views attributed in previous chapters to Adam Smith, Henry Carey and, to some extent, J.S. Mill. That is, Marx's analysis of mineral extraction indicates that in some industries at least, the user cost of extraction may be relatively low. Marx's treatment of the extractive industries with its emphasis on the ease with which output may be expanded is perfectly consistent with his earlier analysis of differential rent in agriculture in which he argues, as Carey had done, that cases of increasing return on the extensive margin are not uncommon. In the next section Marx's case for increasing return on the extensive margin in agriculture is considered.

Return on the Extensive Margin

In discussing the existence of differential rent Marx argues that it 'can develop equally well in a descending sequence which proceeds from better to worse soils, as in an ascending one which progresses in the opposite direction from worse to better soils; or it may be brought about in checkered fashion by alternating movements.'[16] This, says Marx, takes care of the false assumption regarding differential rent found among West, Malthus and Ricardo; namely, that it necessarily presupposes a movement towards worse and worse soil. The precondition for differential rent is merely the inequality of different kinds of soil.[17]

Marx recognises, in this context, that differences in location may be as important as differences in the fertility of the soil but prefers, for the sake of simplicity, to consider only differences in fertility. In so doing, he shows, by a series of numerical examples, the way in which total rent and rent per acre behave as expanded production is met alternatively by extension of soil of the poorest type, by extension of soil of all existing degrees of fertility and finally, by extension of soil of the best type.[18] As well as this abstract consideration of extension of better types of soil, Marx also considers practical reasons why the progress of cultivation may bring equally good or even better soils under the plough.[19]

Firstly, Marx argues, improvements in communications may bring better soils under cultivation. Secondly, developments in natural science and agronomy or developments of ways of overcoming physical obstacles to cultivation may render previously inferior soil superior.[20] Thirdly, institutional changes (such as the release of unworked communal or state-owned lands) may free, for cultivation, previously unavailable land of superior quality. Fourthly, although a large expansion of capital will quickly bring more soil under cultivation and although it is unlikely that this soil will be of more than equal quality with the best soil now cultivated, it is possible that, by chance, some better soil will be developed.

The reasons which Marx gives for the existence of increasing return on the extensive margin in agriculture are clearly similar to those offered by Henry Carey. Taken with the support shown for Carey's position by J.S. Mill, they represent a significant contributing factor to the eventual acceptance of Carey's hypothesis.

Conclusion

As the chapters which follow will make clear, in terms of the mainstream development of the economics of mineral extraction there is only one aspect of Marx's treatment of the topic which is of some significance. This is his implication that some mining activities, at least, are not subject to diminishing return on the extensive margin. In these industries output may be easily expanded.

Marx's idea that at least some of the mineral industries may be easily expanded is consistent with similar optimistic views put forward by Adam Smith, Carey and J.S. Mill. It implies that user cost of present production will be relatively low or zero; that is, that there is little or no antagonism between present and future production. Although this possibility is not greatly emphasised in the contemporary economic treatment of mineral extraction it can be seen from the conclusions drawn by the prominent classical economists whose work has been reviewed in this and the previous chapters that it was an idea that was widely canvassed in the classical literature. Even Ricardo's emphasis on resort to inferior resources is moderated by reference to the increasing return associated with the discovery of the precious metal mines of South America.

Not only does Marx give support for the idea of increasing return in mining, but he also provides one of the better argued cases for Carey's hypothesis of increasing return on the extensive margin in agriculture. In particular, he gives a wide range of reasons for the existence of such a regime.

Notes

1. K. Marx, *Capital* (Progress Press, Moscow, 1954).

2. K. Marx, *Theories of Surplus Value*, G.A.Bonner and E.Burns translators (Lawrence and Wishart, London,1951).

3. K. Marx, *Theories of Surplus Value*, part II (Lawrence and Wishart, London, 1969).

4. Marx, *Capital*, vol. 1, pp. 474-5.

5. In his extensive discussion of Ricardo's theory of rent in *Theories of Surplus Value*, Marx makes it clear that although he is aware of the fact of exhaustibility of mines, he considers it to be irrelevant for the question of whether mine income is rent or not. Marx, *Theories*, ch. 11.

6. Marx, *Capital*, vol. 3, p. 775.

7. This is the passage quoted on p. 56 above.

8. Earlier in *Capital*, Marx refers to this passage as indicative of very specific and accidental cases where *de facto* abolition of landed property occurs (by virtue of the coincidence of the roles of landlord and capitalist) and where, as a result of this abolition, marginal land yields no rent. Marx, *Capital*, vol. 3, pp. 751-2 *et seq.* J.U. Nef later unwittingly lent support for Marx's view that, in normal cases where a non-coincidence of landlord and capitalist exists, the marginal mine will pay a rent. He argued that a system in which royalty payments differed little between mines in spite of significant differences in their fertility had become institutionalised in the United Kingdom. J.U. Nef, *The Rise of the British Coal Industry* (Cass, London, 1966), vol. 1, p. 327.

9. Marx, *Capital*, vol. 3, p. 781.

10. Ibid., p. 772.

11. In discussing the way in which values of commodities are related to their market prices, Marx laid the foundation for what is known today as the 'transformation problem'. In Marx's system, if all commodities were to exchange at prices equal to their values then the organic composition of capital (capital intensity) would have to be the same in every industry. Since the organic composition of capital obviously varies from industry to industry, Marx accommodated this variance by suggesting that commodities do not necessarily exchange at prices equal to their values. Although the aggregate price of society's output will equal aggregate value, in the case of individual commodities price may vary from value. It will do so in a systematic way such that the prices of commodities having an organic composition of capital higher than the societal average will be greater than values, while the prices of commodities having a lower organic composition of capital than the average will be lower than values. The extractive industries come into this second class. It is generally recognised that Marx's solution to the problem of how values are transformed into prices has many unsatisfactory aspects. A succinct review of the transformation problem and the unsatisfactory aspects of Marx's solution to it may be found in T. Bottomore (ed.), *A Dictionary of Marxist Thought* (Blackwell, Oxford, 1983), p. 391.

12. Marx, *Capital*, vol. 3, p. 768. Although Marx here makes no reference to the enigmatic treatment of forestry by Ricardo or to Ricardo's objections to Adam Smith's treatment of the topic, he does so in *Theories of Surplus Value* where he argues that Adam Smith's contention that income from forests and mines is rent is correct and that Ricardo was wrong to argue otherwise. Marx, *Theories*, ch.11.

13. Ibid., pp. 249-50.

14. Marx makes this connection explicitly in *Theories of Surplus Value*. Marx, *Theories*, p. 365.

15. It is clear that Marx is thinking of output being readily expanded in the long run: 'Adam Smith makes a correct distinction here between land and mines, because with the latter he presupposes that there is never a transition to worse sorts - always to better ones - and that they always provide more than the necessary additional supply.' Ibid., p. 338, original emphasis. This passage has also been cited above in the chapter dealing with Adam Smith.

16. Marx, *Capital*, vol. 3, p. 658.

17. Ibid., pp. 658-9. Marx does not acknowledge J.S. Mill who had earlier reached a similar conclusion.

18. Ibid., pp. 661-8.

19. Ibid.

20. Marx cites the example of light soil types in France and England which have, as a result of improvements in agronomy, risen from an inferior rank to become the best soils.

10
W.R. Sorley

In 1889 in the *Journal of the Royal Statistical Society* there was
published a seldom cited paper by W.R. Sorley.[1] This paper which
preceded the first edition of Marshall's *Principles* discusses the
incidence and effects of mining royalties upon the iron and steel
trades of Britain. In his paper, Sorley undertakes, *inter alia*, a
thorough analysis of the rent of mines. This analysis points to the
basis for a royalty payment in the inevitability of exhaustion of the
contents of an operating mine. Although J.S. Mill had already
indicated the possibility of antagonism between present and future
production, it was Sorley who took the next step which involved
linking this idea with the institutionalised system of payment of
royalties to the owners of operating mines - including the marginal
mine.[2]

The subject matter of Sorley's paper was prompted by the
severe depression of the iron and coal trades which occurred in the
1880s; and by the resulting criticism from within those trades of
the prevailing royalty system which was said to have exacerbated
the depression and its ill effects. While Sorley's paper is a long one
(over 14,000 words) much of its content is historical and descriptive and is thus of only passing interest in the context of this
review. There is, however, a thorough treatment of the theory of
mineral rent in the paper and it is this treatment which has
greatest significance for the historical development of the literature
of the economics of exhaustible resources. The first part of this
chapter involves a brief outline of the content of Sorley's article.
This outline is then used in the second and major part of this
chapter as the background for an extensive discussion of Sorley's
analysis of the nature of mineral rent. The third and final part of

this chapter involves a review of Sorley's contribution to the historical development of the economics of exhaustible resources.

Overview of Sorley's Article

Sorley commences his discussion of the effect of royalties on the iron and coal trades with an historical outline of the development, in Britain, of systems of property rights in minerals and of payment of royalties to mine owners. He attributes the nature of the prevailing law to four factors: Roman law; the customs of antiquity; encroachments on existing customs by countervailing laws; and finally, the privilege of the Crown with respect to the precious metals.[3] He points out that although the Roman emperor Gratian introduced a system of *ad valorem* royalties which was of the nature of the modern royalty system, in Britain a similar system developed only slowly over the period from the fourteenth to the eighteenth century.[4]

The next section of Sorley's paper involves a descriptive account of the prevailing arrangements in Britain for the payment to mine owners of rents and royalties. He discusses in turn 'certain' or 'dead' rents, unit royalties and payments for wayleave.[5] Much of this discussion is devoted to detailing the actual values of these rents paid in different parts of the country. In discussing each of these forms of rent Sorley also points briefly to their economic justification.

'Certain' or 'dead' rents which are a fixed, periodic sum paid without regard to the level of production are collected so as to give the landlord an income even if the lessee chooses to leave the mine idle or work it at relatively low levels of output. On the other hand, unit royalties find their justification in the deterioration of the mine which goes with extraction of the mineral. The effect of the landlord levying both 'certain' rents and royalties at the same time is to enable him to have 'an each-way bet':

'The royalty protects the landlord against the rapid exhaustion of the mine, as the certain rent protects him against its lying idle.'[6]

Although Sorley does not make the point specifically the 'certain' rent gives some protection to the landlord against a fall in the capitalised value of his mineral deposit which might occur even if it remains unworked. Under Ricardian assumptions (of resort to inferior resources over time) such a fall in the capitalised value of a mineral deposit is highly unlikely since the deposit becomes increasingly above the margin over time as the margin is determined, *cet. par.*, by increasingly inferior deposits. On the other hand if a Careyan assumption is employed (availability of superior resources over time) a mineral deposit which currently has a capitalised value may, even if it lies idle, experience a fall in that value as it becomes more and more marginal over time. Unlike the Ricardian case, in the Carey case the landlord has much to lose if the lessee does not work his mine.

Can the existence of 'certain' rents thus be taken as prima facie evidence of the real world possibility of a progression to superior resources over time? While thorough consideration of this question lies outside the scope of this study, it is worth noting here that, although 'certain' rents will provide insurance against losses due to an environment in which increasingly superior mineral resources are used over time, they also insure against other losses due, for example, to a downturn in the trade cycle or to the occasional random discovery of superior resources.

The last of the three types of rent discussed by Sorley is payment for wayleave which is remuneration for right of way over or under the surface of land adjacent to that being mined. While Sorley points out that in the case of rents of this type there is much scope for the use of monopoly power, his further discussion of wayleaves is of little relevance here.[7]

In the next section of his paper Sorley describes prevailing attitudes to the contemporary royalty system and concludes that there is universal dissatisfaction with it. He sums up this dissatisfaction under three headings:

'1. That the royalties being measured by a fixed sum of money per quantity of output, weigh with exceptional severity upon the trade whenever it is already in a depressed condition and prices are low.

2. That English trade is placed at a disadvantage, owing to heavy royalties, in competition with foreign countries where the royalty is low or where there is hardly any royalty.

3. That it is "unfair" or "unjust" for the landlord's rent to continue unimpaired when the wages of workmen are being reduced and the profits of employers disappear; and even (as

is frequently argued on platforms) that it is unjust for the landlord to claim any right to the minerals under his land, seeing he did not put them there.'[8]

In the sections of his paper discussed above, Sorley gives the reader a comprehensive picture of the state of the iron and coal trades in Britain and of the role played by royalties in these trades. He does so in order to facilitate his later discussion of suitable reform for the royalty system. Before turning to the question of reform, however, he first discusses at length the theoretical basis for the existence of royalties in the mineral industries. It is this discussion which is of most interest in the context of the development of the economic treatment of mineral extraction; and while it is discussed only briefly in this overview, it is given thorough treatment later in this chapter.

Sorley commences his discussion of mine rent by briefly outlining the standard (Ricardian) theory of agricultural rent. Having done so, he asks whether the rent of mines is, indeed, determined in the same way as the rent of farms. His answer to this question is in the negative - whereas the worst mine (which regulates price) cannot be kept going in the long run, the worst farm can. This feature of mines which necessitates deterioration of the mine as it is worked means that the landlord will suffer a loss if his mine is worked - even if it is the worst mine operating. Thus even the landlord of the worst mine will exact a royalty payment from the mine operator and this royalty or rent which Sorley called the 'minimum' royalty will enter into price.[9]

Sorley's analysis of the rent bearing capacity of mines on the extensive margin is followed by a theoretical discussion of the intensive margin in which he asserts a fundamental difference between mining and agriculture. This fundamental difference which relates to differences in the institutional arrangements for the collection of rents in agriculture and in mining is considered more fully in a later section of this chapter.

Returning to the property of extension of mines, Sorley asks how rents paid by intramarginal mines are determined. In this case, he says, rents are determined by the differential principle in a manner similar to that which applies to agriculture. Like agricultural rent, the effect of the confiscation of differential mine rent will be neutral.[10]

Sorley concludes his section dealing with mineral rents by asking to what extent the theory which he has outlined is reflected in reality. He notes that uncertainty may prevent actual rents from reflecting theoretical values, citing examples of historical periods when (with hindsight) it can be seen that actual rents were above or below their theoretical values. In relation to the theoretical proposition that price will be regulated by the worst mine, Sorley again notes that reality may differ from theory if the more fertile mines are monopolised by large capitalists who affect price by undercutting the operators of marginal mines.[11]

Having discussed the rent of mines, Sorley goes on to consider the effect of royalties on the ability of British mine owners to compete internationally. The major part of this section deals with institutional arrangements on the continent for the working of mines and for payment of associated rents. Sorley concludes that continental royalties are lower than those in Britain and, since the royalty enters into price, continental mines have a competitive advantage over their British counterparts.[12]

From a twentieth century perspective, Sorley's treatment of royalties in the international context is somewhat simplistic. In this context he sees the royalty as simply an imposition on the mine operator, choosing to ignore his argument that it is compensation to the landlord or concessionaire for the depreciation of a valuable asset. No consideration is given to the effect of differing royalties rates in different countries on the time profile of production nor is there any hint of the possible effect of the higher British royalty in retarding British output - thus changing the relative advantage of British mines at some time in the future.

Sorley concludes his paper with a section outlining his proposals for reform in the British iron and coal trades. He considers proposals for nationalisation and for the abolition of royalties, dismissing these in a single paragraph saying that nationalisation is part of the wider issue of whether all landed property should be confiscated.[13]

In relation to the abolition of royalties, Sorley strangely argues that such a change would have serious dislocative effects. In spite of his earlier discussion of the rent of mines in which he argues that the levying of theoretical rents is neutral in its effects, he asserts that abolition will result in a disequilibrium disadvantaging poorer mines in given districts and all mines in the poorer districts.[14] Whether Sorley attributes such dislocation to the variance of actual rents from their theoretical values is not clear. However, his assertion that the abolition of royalties would result in a reduction of price by the full amount of the 'minimum' royalty (the royalty paid by the worst mine) indicates a simplistic theoretical approach. At the time Sorley was writing it was well understood that the burden of a tax does not necessarily fall entirely upon the producer.[15]

Sorley thus concludes that abolition of the royalty will not pose a satisfactory solution to the problems of the iron and steel trades. Its problems, he says, result, *inter alia*, from the system of unit royalties which leaves the royalty unchanged when a depression of trade reduces prices received by mine operators. He suggests, therefore, the introduction of a system of *ad valorem* royalties.[16] Sorley also discusses solutions to the problems posed by the wayleave system but these do not have relevance for this review and are not discussed here.

An overall assessment of Sorley's paper reveals that it offers a thorough and perspicacious analysis of the iron and coal trades in his time - although it does suffer from an oversimplification of the likely effects of the abolition of royalties. Sorley's discussion of the rent of mines has been given only brief consideration in the preceding review of his paper. It is, however, the most important part of his paper insofar as the historical development of the economics of exhaustible resources is concerned. In the next section of this chapter a thorough analysis of Sorley's treatment of mineral rent is undertaken.

The Rent of Mines

Sorley commences his discussion of the rent of mines with the observation that mine rents are usually treated by economists as an appendix to the theory of agricultural rent.[17] He sums up that theory by saying that it proposes that rent does not enter into the price of a product - rather, it is the price of the product which determines rent; and price is determined by costs on the highest cost farm under cultivation.[18] Having reminded the reader that agricultural rents are neutral, Sorley then asks if the abolition of mineral rents would also render no change in equilibrium market price and quantity. He answers that the common view amongst economists is that there would be no change. [19] He offers as evidence for this view the quotation from Ricardo in which he asserts that mineral rents are explained in the same way as are agricultural rents.[20] With equal distinction, says Sorley, the similarity between agricultural and mineral rents is asserted by

Bagehot: 'it is the worst mine which can, in the long run, be kept going that in the long run determines the price of the produce.'[21]

It is Bagehot's notion of mines operating in the long run which Sorley uses as the basis for his discussion of the difference between mineral and agricultural rents. Although the basis for differential rent is the same in the case of mines as in the case of agriculture and although prices will be regulated in mines (as they are in agriculture) by costs in the worst mine, the worst mine cannot be kept going in the long run whereas the worst farm can.[22] While the worst farm will pay no rent, it does not follow that the worst mine will pay none. This is explained by the fact that, although land may be improved by cultivation or at least not deteriorate with use, the worst mine must deteriorate as it is worked. Whereas a landlord would rather have the worst farm cultivated than lie waste, the landlord of the worst mine would rather have it lie idle than have it deteriorate through use unless there is some distinct gain from its being used.[23] By allowing his mine to be worked the landlord of the worst mine 'loses a *possible* future source of income.'[24] Sorley sums up his argument in the following way:

'Hence as mines deteriorate by being worked, the landlord will only let them at a rent bearing some proportion to the amount of deterioration they suffer. Even the least fertile mine worked will pay a rent of this kind, and this rent will enter into the price of the product.'[25]

Sorley's practical explanation of the source of the rent or royalty paid by the worst mine is abundantly clear. It represents the next stage in the development of the economic treatment of mineral extraction following on from Ricardo's identification of the significance of the exhaustible nature of mineral resources as a source of 'rent' and Mill's recognition of the possibility of antagonism between present and future uses of mineral deposits.

It is interesting that in the penultimate quotation above, Sorley speaks of the landlord losing a 'possible' source of future income if his mine is worked. In the discussion of 'certain' rents in the first section of this chapter it was pointed out that a Careyan assumption (of progression to superior resources over time) implies that deposits which are currently economically viable may become obsolete in the future. On the other hand, under a Ricardian assumption (of recourse to inferior resources) the value of a mineral deposit will increase over time. In his discussion of the relevance for the landlord of a decision by a lessee to work his mine, Sorley speaks of the loss of a 'possible' source of future income rather than the loss of a 'certain' or 'probable' source of future income. Can it thus be inferred from Sorley's choice of word that he considers that there is a significant likelihood that a Careyan situation of increasing return on the extensive margin will prevail? Although there are many circumstances - as noted in the discussion of 'certain' rents above - which may lead a landlord to be uncertain about the extent of future income from a mineral deposit even when the Ricardian assumption of diminishing return on the extensive margin holds, Sorley's cautious approach to the likelihood of future income does question the appropriateness of a Ricardian approach.

Having discussed, in a practical fashion, the reasons for the payment of rent to the landlord of a marginal mine, Sorley next undertakes a more theoretical analysis which involves the relationship between rent on the intensive margin of the mine and rent on the intensive margin of the farm.

Citing James Mill and Alfred Marshall as his authorities, Sorley argues that on every farm the presence of diminishing returns guarantees that although the last unit of the variable factor applied to the land will produce a return just equal to its cost, all previously applied units will produce returns in excess of their cost and will thus generate a surplus which is paid as rent. In other words, on every farm it is only the margin or fringe of production which pays no rent.[26] But, says Sorley, this principle does not apply in the case of mines - in mines the last unit of the variable factor employed 'pays as large a share of rent as any other.' [27] Thus, in the short run, the last ton of mineral produced from the individual mine pays the same royalty as the first ton produced.[28] It is at this stage that Sorley makes a curious assertion which, if it is taken at face value, creates doubt in the reader's mind as to the soundness of this theoretical analysis. Having argued that the last ton of mineral will pay the same royalty as the first, Sorley declares:

'The royalty system thus prevents the theory of rent from holding true of mines as it does of agricultural land; and the royalty system itself is rendered necessary by the fundamental difference between a farm and a mine, that the latter is, while the former is not, deteriorated by working.'[29]

Is it to be inferred from this quotation that Sorley believed that economic laws may be rendered inoperative by institutional arrangements (such as those relating to the collection of rent) or is there a less obvious point being made? The system of unit royalties in the mineral industries means that rents are a variable cost in these industries whereas the periodic rents of agriculture are a fixed cost. Now, although production decisions will differ according to whether rent is levied in such a way as to be a fixed or a variable cost, in both agriculture and in mining production is carried out at any point in time with a fixed factor service (land or mineral) and in each case the short run theory of production will apply - subject to the qualifications outlined in chapter 3 above. Only if Sorley is assuming that mining is subject to constant returns in the short run - while agriculture involves diminishing returns - will the theoretical treatment of the intensive margin in mining differ from its treatment in agriculture. Sorley does not, however, so much as hint at the possibility of constant returns in mining; and, unless his statement is simply deemed to be incorrect, an alternative explanation must be sought.[30]

Sorley continues on from the quotation above with a statement explaining that the idea that the royalty system prevents the theory of rent from holding true is sometimes illustrated by saying that income from mines is not rent since royalties are payment for material removed from the mine.[31] Is the above quotation from Sorley thus a roundabout way of simply saying, as Ricardo had done, that mine income is not rent since the basis for income from the mine is impermanent? There are no further clues as to Sorley's intention and the question of whether or not this interpretation is correct is, unfortunately, one which must remain unanswered. The only conclusion which may safely be drawn, therefore, is that Sorley's meaning is unclear.

In spite of Sorley's sometimes confusing treatment of income from the mine, he does make clear the necessity for the operator of the marginal mine to make payment of a 'minimum' royalty to the owner of the mine for its use. This is an idea which was later taken up by Marshall and thoroughly analysed by Lewis Gray. Just as Sorley had done, Marshall argued that the marginal mine will pay a rent or royalty which reflects the cost of the exhaustible mineral used up, and that the marginal supply price of minerals will therefore include the 'minimum' royalty. On the other hand, Gray rejected the idea of the worst mine paying a rent or royalty. He did argue, however, that the mine owner-operator would take into consideration the effect of production in depleting the value of an intramarginal mine and would adjust his output accordingly. It is interesting that although Gray cites Sorley as being a notable protagonist of the view that the marginal mine will yield a royalty, he incorrectly attributes Sorley's justification for this view to the need for compensation of owners of marginal mines for the negative externalities they confer on neighbours by allowing an 'unpopular institution' to operate on their land.[32]

Sorley continues his discussion of the rent of mines by next considering the source of differential royalties (differential rents). In arguing that the 'minimum' royalty paid by the worst mine enters into price and that differential royalties paid by intramarginal mines will thus exceed this 'minimum' royalty depending on their cost advantage in relation to the worst mine, Sorley clearly employs a methodology which is more classical than neoclassical in its approach. For him, differential royalties are price determined rather than price determining.

Noting that for actual royalties to reflect theoretical values there would need to be a competitive environment with no uncertainty, Sorley next discusses the likely effects of imperfect competition on the pricing of the output of the mineral industries. For various reasons, says Sorley, the 'good' mines are monopolised by large capitalists who have the 'chief say in determining prices.'[33] Actual market prices are usually the prices at which the large capitalists can be induced to work and smaller operators must struggle to keep up with them.[34] The outcome of this market structure is that 'although the theoretical or "normal" price is said to be fixed by expenses of production in the poorest mines, the actual or "market" price is determined by a competition in which the workers of these poorer mines have but little say.'[35] Having declared his opinion in no uncertain way, Sorley continues with a somewhat contradictory argument to the effect that although prices are not fixed by conditions in the worst mines, they are still sufficient to allow these mines to continue in operation. Furthermore, although the large capitalists have the chief say in determining prices, costs in the worst mine are, nevertheless, a measure of average prices.[36] Although Smith is not cited, Sorley's role for the more fertile mines in the determination of price is evocative of his treatment in *The Wealth of Nations*. On the other hand, Sorley's role for the more fertile mines depends primarily on the monopoly power of their operators - a factor which Smith does not mention.

Finally, Sorley's discussion of the rent of mines is not only significant for its inclusion of an explanation for the surplus which is said to be yielded by the marginal mine, but it is also of particular significance by virtue of its representing the first thorough treatment of mineral rent in its own right. Presented as it was in the form of a journal article, Sorley's discussion of mine rent was the first such discussion to appear outside the context of a volume devoted to economic principles in general.

Conclusion

Sorley's treatment of mines which represents a significant advance from the work of his classical predecessors is the forerunner of the definitive neoclassical contributions which appeared in the early part of this century. In relation to his predecessors, Sorley's most significant contribution is his explanation of the theoretical foundation for the payment of royalties to the owners of marginal mines. The idea that these payments represent compensation to the owner for deterioration in the value of an asset involves a logical extension of J.S. Mill's idea that there may be an antagonism between present and future production from the mine. Furthermore, by presenting his theoretical conclusions in the context of a thorough review of the British iron and coal trades Sorley was able to give them a plausibility and relevance which, with the exception of the work of Adam Smith, was not matched by his predecessors.

It is clear from Sorley's discussion of justification for royalty payments to owners of mines that he bases his theoretical conclusions on a tacit assumption that increasing scarcity of mineral resources is the norm. That is, he assumes that there is positive user cost of production associated with decreasing return on the extensive margin. This essentially Ricardian premiss is, however, sometimes belied by discussions (such as those relating to 'certain' rents) in which there is a hint of the possibility of a low user cost regime involving a Careyan progression to superior resources.

Finally, in the context of this review, Sorley's economic analysis of mining represents a watershed which divides the work of his classical predecessors from that of his successors who took an increasingly neoclassical approach to analysis of the economics of mineral extraction. In spite of the significance of Sorley's work in this respect, it has gone largely unnoticed in the recent literature.

Notes

1. W.R. Sorley, 'Mining royalties and their effect on the iron and coal trades', *Royal Statistical Society Journal*, vol. 52 (1889). Biographical details of Sorley may be found in the *Dictionary of National Biography*, 1931-40 (Oxford University Press, Oxford), pp. 827-8.

2. F.A. Walker had already discussed this idea but he did not make it clear whether marginal mines would normally pay a royalty. F.A. Walker, *Political Economy*, 3rd edn (Macmillan, London, 1887), p. 215.

3. Sorley, 'Mining royalties and their effect on the iron and coal trades', p. 60.

4. Ibid., pp. 60-1.

5. Ibid., pp. 65-8.

6. Ibid., p. 66.

7. Ibid., p. 68.

8. Ibid., p. 74.

9. Ibid., p. 76.

10. Ibid., pp. 78-9.

11. Ibid., pp. 80-1.

12. Ibid., pp. 86-7.

13. Ibid., p. 88.

14. Ibid., pp. 90-1.

15. For example, see J.S. Mill, *Principles of Political Economy* (Routledge, London, 1895), bk 5, ch. 4.

16. Sorley, 'Mining royalties and their effect on the iron and coal trades', pp. 92-3.

17. Even in the twentieth century much of the literature dealing with the economics of mining does not recognise the exhaustible nature of the natural resource being exploited. For example, I.M.D. Little, in defining the marginal cost of coal, does not ask whether exhaustibility is relevant to his definition. I.M.D. Little, *The Price of Fuel* (Oxford University Press, London, 1953), appendix to ch. 1.

18. Sorley, 'Mining royalties and their effect on the iron and coal trades', p. 75.

19. Ibid.

20. Sorley does not, however, make mention of Ricardo's earlier contradictory treatment of mines in which the destructible nature of the basis for rent is clearly identified.

21. Sorley, 'Mining royalties and their effect on the iron and coal trades', p. 76. The quotation is from Bagehot's *Economic Studies*, no publisher or date given, p. 127.

22. Sorley, 'Mining royalties and their effect on the iron and coal trades', p. 76.

23. Sorley makes it clear that the position he attributes to the landlord of a farm is contingent upon the absence of predatory farming.

24. Sorley, 'Mining royalties and their effect on the iron and coal trades', p. 76, emphasis added.

25. Ibid.

26. Ibid., p. 77.

27. Ibid.

28. Ibid.

29. Ibid.

30. Although Sorley did not mention the nature of short run return in the mine, it is possible that he considered constant return to be the norm. As the next chapter will show, Alfred Marshall asserted that mines experience constant return in the short run.

31. Sorley, 'Mining royalties and their effect on the iron and coal trades', p. 77.

32. L.C. Gray, 'Rent under the assumption of exhaustibility', *Quarterly Journal of Economics*, vol. 28 (1914), reprinted in M. Gaffney (ed.), *Extractive Resources and Taxation* (University of Wisconsin Press, Madison, 1967), p. 438 *n*.

33. Sorley, 'Mining royalties and their effect on the iron and coal trades', p. 80.

34. Ibid.

35. Ibid.

36. Ibid., p. 81.

11

Alfred Marshall

Alfred Marshall's analysis of the economics of mining is, in many respects, similar to Sorley's earlier treatment. Although Marshall's analysis of mining is much briefer than is Sorley's, Marshall's much wider audience meant that his interpretation was much more widely disseminated. As this and subsequent chapters will show, it is Marshall's rather than Sorley's position which is most often quoted by later authors.

Marshall's technique, in considering mines, is similar to J.S. Mill's in that the analysis of mining is typically by way of a 'postscript' to the analytical treatment of agriculture; and in Marshall's case this technique is sometimes even more apparent since he often relegates the discussion of mines to a footnote. Marshall's treatment of agricultural rent is considered to contain more classical content than was warranted in his neoclassical age. Whereas, says Schumpeter, there is no doubt that Marshall accepted the marginal productivity theory of rent, he refused to recognise the break that this represented from Ricardo's position, fighting a 'rearguard action in defence of Ricardo.'[1] Similarly, George Stigler described Marshall as considerably revising the classical theory of rent, arguing that he presented a doctrine which was 'on the whole more classical in spirit than in content.'[2] Whether these assessments are equally valid in the case of Marshall's treatment of mines is a question which is addressed at a later stage in this chapter.

Although Marshall's consideration of mining is brief, it is, nonetheless, pithy - providing much food for thought. While Marshall briefly considered the economics of mining *qua* mining in the *Economics of Industry,* his more thorough treatment occurs in the *Principles* where reference is made to the economics of mining in three different chapters.[3] In the *Principles*, Marshall repeats the limited treatment contained in the *Economics of Industry* and adds significant new material. The text of this chapter considers only the references to the economics of mining which occur in the *Principles*; although, where this treatment echoes that of the *Economics of Industry*, end notes will indicate that this is so. In addition to the discussion of mines in the *Principles*, Marshall also considers Carey's hypothesis of increasing return on the extensive margin in agriculture, and this aspect is also considered later in the chapter.[4] This chapter comprises three sections. In the first, Marshall's analysis of mining is considered; in the second, his attitude to the idea of increasing return on the extensive margin in agriculture is discussed; and in the third, some conclusions are drawn.

The Treatment of Mining

Marshall's first reference to the economics of mines in the *Principles* is one in which he discusses the nature of return. He carefully argues that, *cet. par.*, mining will involve increased difficulty in obtaining further supplies of minerals and will thus display diminishing returns over historical time. He notes that on the other hand, this tendency may be countered by improvements in mining methods and by increased exploration. However, he offers no opinion in the *Principles* as to whether the factors which counter diminishing returns may be sufficiently strong as to cause historically constant or even increasing returns to occur. [5] Marshall continues his investigation of the nature of returns in the industry by noting that the mine differs from agricultural land in that the latter, if 'properly' cultivated, retains its fertility while the former involves the giving up of stored-up treasures.[6] He curiously uses this distinction as the foundation for an argument to the effect that, unlike agricultural lands, mines display constant returns in the short run.

Using an aquatic analogy Marshall argues that whereas agricultural output and the output of fisheries is like a perennial stream, the output of mines is like the flow from a reservoir. Continuing the analogy, he argues that, like a reservoir, as the individual mine becomes deeper (over time) the greater is the unit cost of extraction - although this unit cost is, when the total contents of the mine are considered, independent of the rate of extraction:

'The more nearly a reservoir is exhausted, the greater is the labour of pumping from it, but if one man could pump it out in ten days, ten men could pump it out in one day: and when once empty, it would yield no more. So the mines that are being opened this year might just as easily have been opened many years ago: if the plans had been properly laid in advance, and the requisite specialised capital and skill got ready for the work, ten years' supply of coal might have been raised in one year without any increased difficulty; and when a vein had once given up its treasure, it could produce no more.'[7]

In relation to this quotation it is important to understand that Marshall maintained the classical tradition of treating the mineral deposit as the short run fixed factor. In keeping with the established convention, he considered both capital and labour to be variable factors. That this is so is evidenced by his definition of the law of [short run] diminishing return: 'An increase in the capital and labour applied in the cultivation of land causes *in general* a less than proportionate increase in the amount of produce raised, unless it happens to coincide with an improvement in the arts of agriculture.'[8] Thus when Marshall speaks, in the quotation in the paragraph above, of capital and skill being readied for the extraction of the contents of the mine in one year at similar cost to that incurred in extracting them in ten, he is clearly suggesting constant returns in the short run. Marshall's suggestion that mines experience constant returns in the short run while costs rise with cumulative extraction closely parallels Mill's treatment - although Mill did suggest that some mines are subject to diminishing returns in the short run.

It was earlier remarked that Marshall's distinction between the ongoing fertility of the soil and the exhaustibility of mines was a 'curious' foundation for arguing that mines display short run constant returns. However, some consideration of the natural constraints to production in agriculture and in mining render Marshall's foundation less curious than at first supposed. Marshall was probably thinking of the different physical conditions under which agricultural output may be harvested as compared to the conditions under which mineral output may be wrought. Whereas in agriculture a life cycle is relevant and, *cet. par.*, harvesting will occur periodically at the most profitable stage of the cycle, no such cycle exists in mining and, *cet. par.*, 'harvesting' may profitably occur at any time. Short run diminishing returns occur in agriculture since, *inter alia*, an increased rate of application of variable resources to the fixed quantity of land cannot, in most cases, significantly alter the length of the life cycle; in mining there is no similar impediment.

Marshall's hypothesis of constant returns in the short run is supplemented by an hypothesis of constant returns to scale which is revealed in his later chapter in the *Principles* in which he considers the advantages of production on a large scale in industrial organisations.[9] Having argued that economies of scale of plant and of organisation in railways, tramways and shipping give rise to the view that these activities may be suitably undertaken by the state, Marshall argues that the same does not apply in the case of mines.[10] Although there are some mines which have establishment costs so large that only a large business could bear them, 'the small mine or quarry may fairly be expected, other things being equal, to hold its own against the large one.'[11] Whether or not this hypothesis has been verified in recent history, it remains that it represents one of the earliest explicit considerations of returns to scale in mining in the modern economic literature.

In addition to his discussion of the nature of return, there is a second aspect of mines which Marshall considers in the *Principles*. This is the rent of mines. Marshall's first reference to this aspect occurs in his concluding remarks to the argument for constant short run returns in mining. He argues that the exhaustibility of mines explains why mineral rents are calculated on a different principle from farm rents:

'The farmer contracts to give back the land as rich as he found it: a mining company cannot do this; and while the farmer's rent is reckoned by the year, mining rent consists chiefly of "royalties" which are levied in proportion to the stores that are taken out of nature's storehouse.'[12]

At a later stage in the *Principles* Marshall again makes reference to the rent of mines. This reference occurs in the conclusion to the third of his chapters dealing with marginal costs in relation to values.[13] Marshall states that the principles governing the relationship between costs and values which have been explained in the preceding two chapters are not applicable to mines.[14] He goes on to declare that a mineral royalty is *not* a rent although the latter term is often used; that this is so is explained by the exhaustibility of mines which dictates that at least part of the income which a mine yields is payment for the mineral removed. From this observation, Marshall concludes that 'the marginal supply price of minerals includes a royalty in addition to the marginal expenses of working the mine.'[15] This conclusion is identical with Sorley's and Sorley's lucid explanation of the reasons for it applies equally here.[16]

Marshall continues his discussion of the rent of mines with the following observation:

'Of course the owner desires to receive the royalty without undue delay; and the contract between him and a lessee often provides, partly for this reason, for the payment of a rent as well as a royalty.'[17]

When the meaning of the term 'rent' as used in this quotation is understood, Marshall's intention is clear: Marshall is here alluding to the desire of the landlord to protect himself, by virtue of a contractual 'certain' rent, against the mine lying idle and to also gain compensation, by virtue of the contractual royalty, for removal of the contents of the mine. This is the 'each-way bet' which again was so comprehensively discussed by Sorley as to require no further comment here. Marshall concludes his textual discussion of the rent of mines with the following sentence in which he addresses the theoretical basis for the royalty:

'But the royalty itself on a ton of coal, when accurately adjusted, represents that diminution in the value of the mine, regarded as a source of wealth in the future, which is caused by taking the ton out of nature's storehouse.' [18]

In a note to this sentence, Marshall discusses, *inter alia*, Ricardo's conclusion that rent does not enter into the marginal cost of mineral production. He concludes that although Ricardo was technically correct, 'he ought to have added that if a mine is not practically inexhaustible, the income derived from it is partly rent and partly royalty; and that though the rent does not, the minimum royalty does enter directly into the expenses incurred on behalf of every part of the produce whether marginal or not.'[19]

Although, by describing the theoretical royalty as representing the diminution in the value of the mine, Marshall has made its basis clear, nowhere has he explained the basis for the theoretical rent which he says constitutes the other part of the income derived from a mine. Is Marshall thinking of the rent as being differential rent (differential royalty) as defined by Sorley? That is, is Marshall's rent the 'surplus' over and above the minimum royalty (earned by the marginal mine) which accrues to intramarginal mines? Certainly this is Taussig's interpretation.[20] Although this interpretation has gained some currency it is, however, unlikely to be correct; for, the 'surplus' which accrues to the more fertile mines is simply a reflection of the superior resources which are being taken out of nature's superior 'storehouses'. That is, the 'surpluses' earned by these mines - over and above the minimum royalty - are simply a further royalty or differential royalty. That Marshall was aware of this is indicated by his statement that 'the royalty...when accurately adjusted, represents that diminution in the value of the mine...which is caused by taking the ton out of nature's storehouse'. Nowhere in this statement does Marshall suggest that it is only 'surpluses' earned by marginal mines which he has a mind to call royalties. Further evidence that Marshall considered that the 'surplus' earned by intramarginal mines should be called royalty rather than rent is contained in the definition of royalty which is implicit in part of his explanation of quasi-rent. Speaking of the need to make good the wear and tear of improvements on agricultural land before quasi-rent is calculated, he says: 'That part of income which is required to cover wear-and-tear bears some resemblance to a royalty, which does no more than cover the injury done to a mine by taking ore out of it.' [21]

If Marshall's rent which accrues in addition to the royalty is not differential rent (differential royalty), what other explanation can be given for it? It was earlier noted that Marshall points out that mine owners often require payment of a contractual periodic rent ('certain' rent) - partly for the reason that it enables them to receive the contractual royalty without undue delay. It is likely that a component of this 'certain' rent is what Marshall had in mind when arguing that part of the income of the mine is theoretical rent as opposed to theoretical royalty. Marshall states that part of the reason for the levying of this 'certain' rent is to enable owners to receive the royalty without delay but he does not explain the remaining part. A likely explanation for the remaining part is that it is rent for the site value of the land or other resources associated with the mine. Marshall gave some thought to the idea of composite rents and in dealing with them in the *Principles* he argues that, although, in practice, it is often difficult to separate the different rents due to different economic agents working in conjunction with each other, '[t]he corresponding rents can always be distinguished analytically, and sometimes they can be separated commercially.'[22] Although no definite conclusion can be drawn as to the source of the theoretical rent (as opposed to theoretical royalty) which Marshall says is part of the income from the mine, the interpretation that it is that part of the contractual 'certain' rent which derives from the use of economic agents other than the contents of the mine seems most plausible. The question remains, however, whether in some cases the whole of the 'certain' rent is not, at least theoretically, a royalty since, as Marshall points out, the 'certain' rent may be levied for the reason that it enables the mine owner to receive royalties without delay.

As stated in the introduction to this chapter, Marshall's treatment of mines is similar to Sorley's - although much less comprehensive. Apart from the questionable hypothesis of constant returns in the short run and the suggestion of constant returns to scale, it adds little to Sorley's treatment; its significance in the context of the development of the economic theory of mineral extraction lies in the authority of its author and the wide dissemination of his work.

Marshall's treatment of mines is more classical than neoclassical in emphasis and this is well illustrated by the distinction which he makes between mines and agriculture. As Schumpeter points out, Marshall's insistence that a royalty is not a rent violates his own definition of rent as 'income derived from the ownership of land and other free gifts of nature.'[23] Furthermore, says Schumpeter, Marshall denied that royalties are rents 'on the untenable ground that royalties do enter into the price of the mineral mined in a sense other than that in which does the rent of agricultural land.'[24] Although Schumpeter's interpretation of Marshall's grounds for arguing that a royalty is not a rent is excessively restrictive (Marshall's fundamental ground is, like Ricardo's, that the basis for the royalty is a destructible resource) he is making the important point that Marshall has not, in this respect, taken up the neoclassical view that the rent of natural agents, whether destructible or not, does enter into price (is price determining).[25] In relation to mines, Marshall's classical emphasis is best exemplified by his statement that 'the minimum royalty does enter directly into the expenses incurred on behalf of every part of the produce, whether marginal or not.'[26] There is no suggestion here that the differential royalty (as opposed to the 'minimum' royalty paid by the marginal mine) enters into price. [27]

Finally, Marshall declares that his whole argument relating to mineral rents and royalties assumes the conditions of an old country. He says that Taussig is probably right when he doubts that, in a new country, the owner of the marginal mine can secure any payment for its use, assuming that he has incurred no expenditure on it.[28] In the context of this review, Marshall's admission that under certain circumstances the marginal mine may not yield a royalty is of some significance; it indicates that Marshall recognised that although user cost is relevant under certain conditions (those of an old country) this is not always the case. Thus, the idea that the mineral industries are not always characterised by recourse to inferior resources which was suggested by Adam Smith and reiterated by Carey, Mill and Marx has been perpetuated by Marshall - even if, at this stage, it is relegated to the concluding paragraph of a footnote. In the next section of this chapter, Marshall's consideration of Carey's hypothesis of increasing return on the extensive margin in agriculture is briefly discussed.

Increasing Return in Agriculture

Marshall's consideration of historically increasing return is in similar vein to that of J. S. Mill - although Marshall's discussion is much more comprehensive. To consider Marshall's confirmation of Carey's hypothesis in detail would involve going over much of the ground already covered in previous chapters and this discussion is therefore brief.

Marshall's discussion of increasing return on the extensive margin is detailed and comprehensive involving discussion of a great number of contributing factors in a wide range of agricultural pursuits. Most of the discussion is offered as an impartial analysis of the nature of returns in agriculture rather than as verification of Carey's position or as evidence against Ricardo. It is only in the concluding stages of the discussion that Marshall specifically considers the attacks by Carey and others on Ricardo, arguing that they have some solid substance in them.[29] Although Marshall gives little explicit credit to Carey for his part in the development of the hypothesis of increasing return on the extensive margin, his support for Carey's position in this matter is implicit in the extensive evidence he gives in its favour.[30]

In the heyday of Marshall's *Principles* when growth in real output per capita had controverted the dismal prognoses of Malthus and Ricardo, the optimistic hypothesis of increasing return on the extensive margin which Carey and others had proposed was readily assimilated into the mainstream literature. Nowhere is this more evident than in Alfred Marshall's acceptance and refinement of the idea.

Conclusion

A fairly comprehensive assessment of Marshall's contribution to the development of the economics of mineral extraction has already been offered in the concluding remarks to the first section of this chapter. This assessment revealed the eclectic nature of Marshall's treatment of mines which reflects both Ricardo's emphasis on the impermanent basis for 'rent' in mines and Sorley's explanation of the royalty yielded by the marginal mine. Eclectic though Marshall's treatment may be, it does not take up the idea of the need for the individual mine owner to determine an optimum time profile of production. This idea, which was suggested by Mill, was, however, taken up by Lewis Gray whose contribution is considered in the next chapter.

In general, Marshall's analysis of mining is static in nature and although this emphasis may be explained by his overriding objective of distinguishing the fundamental difference between mining and agriculture, it nonetheless contrasts with his thorough analysis in the *Principles* of the dynamics of many of the prominent branches of industry including agriculture.

Notes

1. J.A. Schumpeter, *History of Economic Analysis* (George, Allen and Unwin, London, 1954), p. 934.

2. G.J. Stigler, *Production and Distribution Theories* (Macmillan, New York, 1946), p. 87.

3. A. Marshall, *The Economics of Industry*, 3rd edn (Macmillan, London, 1885). A. Marshall, *Principles of Economics*, 8th edn, 1949 resetting (Macmillan, London, 1920). The ninth (variorum) edition of the *Principles* reveals that various small changes were made to the discussions of mines during Marshall's lifetime. Where these changes are relevant to an appraisal of Marshall's contribution they will be noted. Otherwise, the text of the eighth edition may be taken to be representative

of that of the first which was published in 1890. Marshall also considered mining here and there in his much later *Industry and Trade*; however, no significant new material was added. A. Marshall, *Industry and Trade* (Macmillan, London, 3rd edn 1920), first published in 1919.

4. In the *Principles*, Marshall also reiterates Adam Smith's contention that in a risky trade the chance of great gain leads to excessive investment and correspondingly low returns to the average investor. While acknowledging Smith, Marshall does not, however, indicate that Smith considered that this situation characterised the gold mining industry. Marshall, *Principles*, 8th edn, p. 332.

5. Ibid., pp. 138-9. In the *Economics of Industry* Marshall makes it clear that he considers these factors to be too weak to prevent the supremacy of diminishing returns. *Economics of Industry*, p. 25.

6. Marshall, *Principles*, 8th edn, pp. 138-9.

7. Ibid., p. 139. Marshall also makes this point in the *Economics of Industry*, p. 25. Anthony Scott's interpretation of Marshall's reasons for using the analogy of a reservoir seems misplaced. Speaking of an assumption of his own model of extraction which involves constancy of extraction conditions through time, Scott 'presumes' that Marshall chose the analogy of a reservoir since he was thinking of the extraction of fluid reserves such as those in a well, where conditions of constant cost over time would hold approximately. Scott goes on to 'correct' this interpretation he has made of Marshall's position by arguing that in the case of a well, costs would rise rather than be constant over time since pumping from greater depths involves raising the liquid a greater distance and thus involves greater cost. He continues: 'The reader neverthless is asked to adopt Marshall's assumption that the [short run] cost curve of extraction does not shift in response to the *cumulative* amount that has already been extracted.' (original emphasis) Scott's interpretation of Marshall is clearly contrary to Marshall's intention; for, Marshall is speaking of short run cost curves of extraction which do shift upwards as cumulative extraction occurs but for which the extent of the upward shifts is independent of the rate of extraction of the whole of the contents of the mine. A.T. Scott, 'The theory of the mine under conditions of certainty' in M. Gaffney (ed.), *Extractive Resources and Taxation* (University of Wisconsin Press, Madison, 1967), pp. 27-8. Marshall's explanation of constant return in the short run has also been discussed in a different context in Chapter 3 above.

8. Marshall, *Principles*, 8th edn, p. 125, original emphasis.

9. Ibid., bk 4, ch. 11.

10. Ibid., pp. 241-2.

11. Ibid., p. 242. Although Marshall does not make the point explicitly, it may be assumed that he is considering differences in cost as between small and large *in situ* mineral deposits; for, if he were not, this statement does no more than reiterate the earlier argument for the independence of extraction costs from the rate of extraction.

12. Marshall, *Principles*, 8th edn, p. 139. At the end of this sentence the reader is referred to the following note: 'As Ricardo says (*Principles*, chap II.) "The compensation given (by the lessee) for the mine or quarry is paid for the value of the coal or stone which can be removed from them, and has no connection with the original or indestructible powers of the land." But both he and others seem sometimes to lose sight of these distinctions in discussing the law of diminishing return in its application to mines. Especially is this the case in Ricardo's criticism of Adam Smith's theory of rent (*Principles*, chap. XXIV.).' What Marshall means when he says that Ricardo and others 'seem sometimes to lose sight of these distinctions' is unclear. However, in chapter 24 of his *Principles* Ricardo says that if Adam Smith had understood the nature of the determination of the rent of land

he 'would have made no distinction between the law which regulates the rent of mines and the rent of land.' Perhaps Marshall's criticism of Ricardo is directed at his claiming that the rent of mines is determined in the same way as the rent of land although he understood (but lost sight of) the idea that the basis for each is different? See D. Ricardo, *Principles of Political Economy and Taxation* (Dent, London, 1911), p. 220.

13. Marshall, *Principles*, 8th edn, bk 10, ch. 5.

14. Ibid., p. 364.

15. Ibid. Marshall also makes this point in his journal article dealing with rent. A. Marshall, 'On rent', *Economic Journal*, vol. 3 (1893), reprinted in A. Marshall, *Principles of Economics*, 9th edn (Macmillan, London, 1961), editorial notes, p. 506 *n*.

16. In his first and second editions of the *Principles*, Marshall cited Sorley's paper as an alternative source of this viewpoint. Marshall, *Principles*, 9th edn, editorial notes, p. 440. J.U. Nef gives an altogether different and somewhat implausible explanation of Marshall's hypothesis that royalties enter into marginal supply price. Having argued that, by Marshall's time, royalties no longer reflected the relative fertility of different mines but had become an equal charge on all mines, Nef proposes that 'Marshall saw that royalties are now largely independent of the fertility of the seams, and held that they therefore enter into the selling price of coal, "in addition to the marginal expenses of working the mine".' Nef is here attributing to Marshall the view that since marginal mines are no longer royalty free - as a result of the evolution of a system of uniform royalties - the marginal cost of coal includes the uniform royalty. Nef attributes a similar motive to Sorley who argued that the royalty system prevents the theory of rent holding true of mines. Although the attribution to Sorley may, on account of his confusing treatment of the subject, have some substance, it is unlikely that Marshall was thinking of anything but the theoretical as opposed to institutional relevance of the royalty. See J.U. Nef, *The Rise of the British Coal Industry* (Cass, London, 1966), pp. 328-9.

17. Marshall, *Principles*, 8th edn, p. 364. This sentence first appeared in the fifth edition (1907) and thus predates Lewis Gray's later discussion of the relationship between rent and royalty (discussed in chapter 12 below). See Marshall, *Principles*, 9th edn, editorial notes, p. 439.

18. Marshall, *Principles*, 8th. edn, p. 364.

19. Ibid., *n*. The 'minimum' royalty to which Marshall refers is clearly the 'minimum' royalty which Sorley had earlier identified as being paid by the marginal mine.

20. F.W. Taussig, *Principles of Economics*, 3rd edn (Macmillan, New York, 1923), vol. 2, p. 102.

21. Marshall, *Principles*, 8th edn, p. 354 *n*.

22. Ibid., p. 375.

23. Schumpeter, *History*, p. 935.

24. Ibid., *n*.

25. A similar criticism is offered by Cassel. G. Cassel, *The Theory of Social Economy*, 2nd edn (Harcourt, Brace, New York, 1932), pp. 295-6.

26. Marshall, *Principles*, 8th edn, p. 364 *n*.

27. This interpretation should, however, be considered only in conjunction with Marshall's discussion of the fundamental similarity of 'scarcity rents' and 'differential rents'. Ibid., pp. 351-2.

28. Writing at a time when conservationist sentiment was strong in the United States, Taussig was uncharacteristically optimistic about the future availability of mineral resources. While this optimism was consistent with his view that the marginal mine would not ordinarily yield a surplus, Taussig failed to make this connection himself. F.W. Taussig, *Principles*, 3rd edn, vol. 2, pp. 92-96.

29. Ibid., p. 136. There is also brief consideration of Carey in similar vein in *The Economics of Industry*, p. 24.

30. Marshall also clearly understood that inversion of the rank ordering of land may occur in the short run but did not make af Heurlin's mistake of suggesting that the possibility of such an inversion verifies Carey's hypothesis of historically increasing return. Marshall, *Principles*, 8th edn, p. 131.

12

L.C. Gray

This chapter considers the contribution of the American L.C. Gray to the development of the economics of mineral extraction. Gray's contribution is contained in two papers which were published in the second decade of this century. The first of these, which dealt primarily with the conservation issue, was published in 1913 and contains a brief account of some of the important aspects of the economics of mineral extraction;[1] the second, which was published in the following year, was more theoretical and dealt exclusively with the economics of mineral extraction - building on the brief account given in the earlier paper.[2]

Although Gray was, after Marshall and Taussig, the next English speaking economist to give particular consideration to the economics of mining, part of his work involves a significant debt to the Austrian E.V. Bohm-Bawerk. Although he mentioned mining only in passing as a way of elucidating his general theory of the return from durable goods, Bohm-Bawerk was responsible for a break from the Ricardian tradition which was later used by Gray as the basis for a solution to the long-standing debate as to whether mine surplus is rent or royalty.[3]

In arguing that the theoretical tripartite division of factors of production in the classical system should be supplanted by a bipartite one in which land (natural agents) and capital were theoretically members of the same class of durable goods, Bohm-Bawerk was to lay the foundation for Gray's solution to the long-standing debate as to the significance of the difference between returns attributable to 'indestructible' agricultural lands (rents) and those attributable to 'destructible' mineral deposits (royalties).[4] Bohm-Bawerk's *Positive Theory of Capital* in which he argues for the bipartite division by using the example of a quarry to illustrate the similarity between 'indestructible' and 'destructible' resources (between agricultural lands and mines) was first published in Austria in 1888[5] - prior to the publication of Sorley's paper and prior to the first edition of Marshall's *Principles*; however, in the English speaking world, it followed hot on the heels of these works; Smart's translation being first published in 1891.

Although, as this chapter will show, the significance of Bohm-Bawerk's thesis for Gray's analysis of mineral extraction is acknowledged by Gray himself, it is important to indicate at this stage the substance of Bohm-Bawerk's contribution and to remind the reader that it was disseminated over twenty years before the publication of Gray's work. Nowhere is the substance of Bohm-Bawerk's contribution more succinctly put than in the translator's preface to the 1891 edition of the *Positive Theory of Capital*. Paraphrasing the significance of the conclusions drawn by Bohm-Bawerk in his chapters dealing with interest from durable goods,[6] his translator, William Smart, says that:

'Ricardo in pointing to the "original and indestructible powers of the soil" as the cause of rent, was right so far as his explanation indicated why the gross return was also the net, but wrong so far as it indicated that rent was due to the productiveness of this peculiar kind of durable good. The interest on a mine and the rent from land are essentially the same, although the one should wear out in thirty years while the other is "indestructible".'[7]

Bohm-Bawerk argued that the gross return from a mine was partly a depreciation charge which reflected the fall in the value of the mine which occurred as production occurred, and partly a residual net return which was interest on its capitalised value. This net return or interest on the mine was essentially the same as the net return from indestructible land or any other durable good - be it 'original' or man-made. However, in the case of the indestructible qualities of land, the net return is also the gross since, by definition, there can be no depreciation of indestructible elements. In arguing the case for the inclusion of net returns from all durable goods within the same class, Bohm-Bawerk was the first of the neoclassical authors to argue that the economic treatment of mineral extraction involved the selfsame principles as those which were relevant to any other productive activity; and, in passing, it is interesting that some sixty years later George Stigler

found it necessary to refute arguments to the contrary in concluding 'that there is no general analytical distinction between exhaust-
ing and other resources.'[8]

Although Bohm-Bawerk classified the interest on a mine in the
same way as rent of land, he did not enquire into the status of the
mine's depreciation charge which represents the remaining part of
its gross return. This part of the gross return is a return to the
original but destructible natural resource which constitutes the
contents of the mine; and Ricardo's question of whether or not it
should be put on the same footing as agricultural rent is one which
was not tackled by Bohm-Bawerk, but was later addressed by Gray
who used Bohm-Bawerk's methodology.

Gray's earlier (1913) paper dealing with the relevance of
economics for conservation does contain a brief treatment of the
economics of mineral extraction; however, this treatment is much
less comprehensive than that given in the later (1914) paper which
dealt exclusively with mineral economics. For this reason, in
analysing and assessing Gray's contribution to the development of
the economics of mineral extraction, this chapter will concentrate
on his later paper - although reference will be made to instances
where aspects of his analysis in this paper can be elucidated by
reference to the earlier one.

This chapter commences with a discussion of the way in which
Gray explained the *raison d'etre* for his analysis of the economics
of mining in the opening remarks of his later, mineral economics
paper. This discussion sets the scene for an analysis of Gray's
treatment of the decision making behaviour of the profit maximising mine owner-operator, after which his more general treatment
of various aspects of mineral extraction - including the question of
whether mine income is rent or royalty - is discussed. Finally, some
concluding remarks are offered.

Indestructibility and Ricardian Rent

Although it is Harold Hotelling's 1931 paper which is most
often cited as the seminal work in the modern literature of the
economics of mineral extraction, Lewis Gray had clearly defined
the essential difference between the micro-economics of mining
and that of agriculture or manufacturing in his mineral economics
paper which was published some 17 years earlier.[9] Gray undertook
the first thorough analysis of the difference between the mine
owner-operator's profit maximising decisions and those of the

cultivator of land. This analysis was undertaken in order to help determine, *inter alia*, whether the established Ricardian view of rent as payment for an 'original and indestructible' property was correct. In the introductory remarks to his mineral economics paper, Gray argues that if it can be shown that indestructibility is not a characteristic which separates rent from other forms of income then a new definition of rent may be established - a definition which transcends indestructibility as its sole source.[10]

Gray commences his discussion of the role of indestructibility by noting that there is no basis for rent which could not conceivably lose its utility (be 'destroyed'). He says, however, that in common usage in the literature of economics the term indestructibility has a much more specific meaning than it has in everyday use. What is meant is that a natural agent may have a property for which rent is paid and which is not impaired by use. While in theory, indestructibility may be so defined, in reality, says Gray it is not always possible to isolate returns to indestructible properties from those due to some form of exhaustion. For example, in the case of mines, rent due to the exhaustion of the mineral cannot be separated from that due to the site value of the land.[11] Agricultural land which is exploited under frontier conditions poses similar problems. Since it is frequently impossible to distinguish Ricardian rent from income due to exhaustion and since true Ricardian rent is relevant to only a small part of the total of natural objects, Gray argues that a new concept of rent which transcends indestructibility is required.

Gray goes on to discuss the fundamental difference between natural objects for which prevention of exhaustion is economical (for example, most agricultural lands) and those for which it is not (for example, minerals). He says that agricultural land resembles labour in the sense that it perishes through non-use rather than through use. If agricultural land is capable of productive use year after year, then failure to utilise it involves a loss in the same way that labour suffers a loss through unemployment. On the other hand, failure to extract mineral from a mineral deposit means only that the benefit which may have been derived from its use today must be postponed until some time in the future. Although there is a subtle difference in emphasis, this is essentially the point made by Sorley in his justification for the payment of a royalty in the case of marginal [and intramarginal] mines.[12] (However, as will be shown later, Gray surprisingly considered that it is only intramarginal mines which have a capitalised value that may be the source of a royalty payment.)

The fact that present and future production from the mine are antagonistic means, says Gray, that it is possible that, unlike cases where the source of income is indestructible, maximising behaviour will involve postponement of present production. If, for example, output prices are rising or factor costs are falling while price expectations are positive, there will be an incentive to postpone present production.[13] On the other hand, if output prices are falling or factor costs are rising, there will be an incentive to increase present production.[14]

Although Gray recognises that falling output prices will, *cet. par.*, increase the attractiveness of present production, he does not consider the case where falling output prices mean that the mine will be abandoned before exhaustion occurs; that is, the case where falling output prices mean that, *cet. par.*, the mine will experience economic (as opposed to physical) exhaustion because prices have fallen below (avoidable) cost. In this case, which has been discussed in earlier chapters and which has been most closely identified with the work of H.C. Carey, present and future production might not be antagonistic and failure to undertake current production may involve a loss similar to that incurred by non-use of agricultural land or labour. Gray's perpetuation of the emphasis in the literature on the high user cost of mineral extraction is further discussed at later stages in this chapter.

Having introduced the idea that production decisions in the mine must differ from those in agriculture, Gray next considers the specific nature of these differences by using what he considers to be typical examples of revenues and costs faced by the mining firm in the short run.

Profit Maximisation in the Mine

The initial treatment of the nature of decision making in the mine which Gray undertakes in his mineral economics paper involves a number of key assumptions two of which are tacit in this paper although they were made explicit in his earlier, conservation paper.[15] The first of these tacit assumptions is that the contents of the mine have a capitalised value; the second, that output prices are expected to remain constant. A third assumption which is made explicit in the mineral economics paper is that returns to cumulative production are constant.[16]

Finally, Gray explicitly makes a more general assumption about the nature of the institutional environment relevant to his analysis - an assumption of a type which is seldom made explicit in the modern theoretical literature. This assumption is that ownership of minerals is vested in private individuals who may exploit the mine themselves or lease it such that their own advantage is maximised.[17] In his analysis of short run production in the mine, Gray assumes that coal is the mineral being mined and proceeds on the basis that the mine owner exploits the mine himself; that is, that he is an owner-operator.

Gray commences his discussion of short run production by reminding the reader that the traditional theory suggests that, given short run diminishing returns, a land owner will, in order to maximise his rental return (per time period), work his fixed area of land by adding units of the variable factor up to the point where the marginal product of the last unit is just equal to its cost. But, says Gray, in the case of the mine, the exhaustibility of its contents dictates a different course of action for the owner. Rather than choosing that level of output for which profit *per time period* is maximised (where marginal revenue equals marginal extraction cost) the mine owner may, if he chooses not to discount future returns, limit output in each period to that level for which average cost of extraction is a minimum; that is, to that level which maximises profit *per unit of output*. In this way, the mine owner will maximise the total return from the finite contents of the mine:

> 'If [the mine owner] is willing to wait for the return from his coal, he can postpone for future removal all coal over and above that amount which can be removed at a minimum average expense per ton.'[18]

On the other hand, the farmer will find that it is worth his while to maximise net return per time period by exceeding the level of output for which average cost is a minimum since present and future production are not antagonistic and the production of extra output today does not affect the quantity of future output which may be produced. Gray goes on to use a tabular, arithmetic example to illustrate that a decision to maximise net return per unit of output results in a lower rate of extraction than would occur if a maximum net return per time period were desired.[19]

Having used the simplest of models to illustrate that short run maximising behaviour in the mine differs from that on the farm,

142

Gray proceeds to modify his analysis in order to give it greater realism. His first modification involves the introduction of a discount on the future. Again using a tabular, arithmetic example he shows that, *cet. par.*, a positive rate of interest will, by increasing the attractiveness of present production, cause the owner to tilt the time profile of production towards the present. The mine owner is faced, says Gray, with an antagonism between short run diminishing return which discourages increased production in the present and the discount on the future which encourages it. The outcome of these opposing forces is illustrated by his tabular example which shows that the ideal rates of utilisation are determined by marginalist principles and involve the equalisation of the present value of the net return in each period. Ideal rates of utilisation are shown to be such that output per time period declines over the life of the mine - involving the application of smaller quantities of the variable factor services in the later periods.[20] Although Gray did not specifically consider the effect of *changes* in positive discount rates in his mineral economics paper, he had already done this in his conservation paper where he concluded that higher rates will bring production forward in time.[21]

The next modification which Gray makes to his simple extraction model allows some tentative qualitative conclusions to be made about the effects of relaxation of the assumption that returns to cumulative extraction are constant. He concludes that if there are decreasing returns to cumulative extraction the mine owner's behaviour will be similar to that in an environment of constant returns; while if increasing returns prevail a more marked tilt towards present production 'might' be warranted.[22] Gray offers no rigorous explanation for these conclusions.

Returning to his technique involving tabular, arithmetic examples, Gray next considers the effect upon production decisions of a discrete change in the present and expected future price of the mineral output. Whereas, earlier in his paper, Gray had considered the effects of secular change in present and expected future prices, in this case he is concerned with the effect of a once and for all change in current and expected future prices. He shows that so long as there is a discount on the future, the effect of a permanent rise in output price is to increase the desirability of present production, thus shortening the life of the mine by tilting the time profile of production further towards the present.[23]

Gray concludes his discussion of short run profit maximisation in the mine by noting that although an increase in price will increase the current rate of production in the same way as it does according to the 'Ricardian theory' [of agricultural production], the rate of production in the mine cannot theoretically increase to the rate where marginal product of the variable factor is just equal to its cost (where marginal revenue equals marginal extraction cost). For, says Gray, 'however long the period of utilization may be and however large the discount on the future may become, the net return from the removal of coal at the point of time most remote in the future can never become zero.'[24] That is, present production must always involve user cost.

While this conclusion is, of course, perfectly consistent with Gray's assumption that the finite contents of the mine have a capitalised value, it is clearly possible for production to occur according to the 'Ricardian theory' if present and future production are not antagonistic; and present and future production might not be antagonistic if, *cet. par.*, falling output prices mean that the mine will be abandoned before its finite contents are exhausted.[25]

Throughout Gray's analysis of short run decision making in the mine he invokes the law of diminishing return.[26] He does so in the light of a disconcerting detour into the nature of short run return which he makes in the early stages of his analysis of short run decision making. In this detour he refers to the opinion of some authors - notably Alfred Marshall - that mines do not experience short run diminishing return. Quoting Marshall's use of the analogy of a reservoir to argue for constant returns, Gray says that although constant return may occur in some cases it is 'fairly safe to assume that, as a general rule to which there may be certain exceptions, the law of diminishing productivity is applicable to mining as well as to agriculture.'[27] This conclusion of Gray's is of particular significance in the context of the development of the economics of mineral extraction; and before moving on to the next section, which deals with the extensive margin, the significance of this conclusion and of the treatment of the intensive margin in general will first be discussed.

Within the modern economics literature, it was J.S. Mill who first explicitly indicated the possibility of the mine owner postponing production from an operating mine on account of an inherent antagonism between present and future production. This possibility was not explicitly taken up again until the publication of Gray's two papers dealing with the conservation issue and with mineral economics. While the idea that, in the mine, present and future mineral output may be antagonistic has presumably been widely understood since early times (indeed, this antagonism may be seen to be implicit in the idea that the mine owner exploits a finite, exhaustible resource) it was not the subject of thorough economic analysis until the publication of Gray's work; and in this originative work, Gray offered a comprehensive treatment of the subject which constituted a quantum leap from the work of earlier economists who had discussed the economics of mineral extraction.

Many of Gray's conclusions about the maximising behaviour of the mine owner rely on the relevance for mining of short run diminishing return, and these conclusions were possible only because of Gray's unprecedented assertion that diminishing return was the norm.[28] That Gray needed, in the second decade of this century, to assert the case for short run diminishing return in mining is indicative of the extent to which the economic treatment of mining lagged behind that of agriculture. However, his assertion of that case and the novel conclusions which it allowed him to draw were responsible for a significant advance in the status of the mineral economics literature. The next aspect which Gray considers in his mineral economics paper is the nature of the extensive margin.

The Extensive Margin

In the mineral economics literature, the aspect of Gray's work which has elicited most critical comment is his treatment of the extensive margin. Whereas his analysis of the intensive margin is considered to be noncontroversial and consistent with the principles of neoclassical capital theory, his treatment of the extensive margin has been the source of some criticism.

In his introductory remarks to the treatment of the extensive margin Gray argues that although the assumption of exhaustibility means a significant change in the treatment of the intensive margin, in the case of the extensive margin the assumption 'does not greatly change the Ricardian formula. It is likely that an extension of the margin will occur whenever such an extension is sufficient to repay the expense of removal.'[29] This conclusion is, of course, contrary to those of Sorley and Marshall who both argued that mines on the extensive margin will, by having revenues in excess of their extraction costs, yield a royalty which compensates the owner for the reduction in the value of his mine. The idea that the marginal mine may yield a royalty cannot be true theoretically, says Gray, 'since the coal in the mine on the margin which yields no rent...has no value which could be made the basis of a charge for depreciation.'[30] It is interesting that in making this observation, Gray does note some conditions under which the mine on the extensive margin which currently yields no surplus may yield one in the future. He argues that, if output prices are expected to increase, a future surplus may appear - and this [expected] future surplus may be the source of a current capitalised value for the mine on the extensive margin. That is, a future surplus may, by virtue of its giving a capitalised value to the contents of the marginal mine, form the basis of a depreciation charge or royalty in the present.[31] Gray does not further pursue this possibility of an expectation of rising output prices and it is clear from the remainder of his paper that he considers it to be an unlikely state of affairs.

It was earlier noted that Gray assumes constant output prices. This assumption, taken with his cursory treatment of the possibility of rising output prices as a source of a capitalised value for the mine, indicates a position in relation to the secular trend of prices which is at variance with the one which has been widely accepted in the neoclassical literature ever since the publication of Hotelling's 1931 paper. Indeed, in Hotelling's paper emphasis is placed on the capitalised value of the mine as the source of rises in output price. Not only is Gray's position concerning the likelihood of rising output prices inconsistent with the later neoclassical literature, it may also be construed as being inconsistent with his own treatment of the intensive margin. For, if some mines are to have a capitalised value as Gray assumes while, *cet. par.*, output prices remain constant over time, only some particular assumptions about the nature of the extensive margin will reconcile these two features; and there is no suggestion from Gray that he had these particular assumptions in mind. (These assumptions are later discussed in the conclusion to this chapter.)

In terms of the historical development of the economics of mineral extraction, Gray's insistence on the absence of a surplus on the extensive margin represents a retrograde step. The likelihood of such a surplus and the reasons for it which were earlier canvassed by both Sorley and Marshall have become basic features of the modern economic treatment of mineral extraction.[32]

In the introduction to this chapter, Gray's debt to the work of Bohm-Bawerk was discussed. It was there revealed that, although Bohm-Bawerk had satisfactorily assimilated the net returns to both exhaustible and indestructible natural resources into the general class of returns to durable goods of all types, in the case of exhaustible resources he had not addressed the question of the way in which the remainder of the gross return - the depreciation charge on the mine - should be classified.

The question of the nature of the return to exhaustible natural resources which was first raised by Ricardo, was one which involved the problem of whether this return was rent like the return to indestructible land or was something else. Amongst those who argued that it was something else was Alfred Marshall who described the return as a royalty and explained it, as Sorley had done, as compensation for mineral removed - as a depreciation charge. Although Bohm-Bawerk successfully fulfilled his major objective of indicating the similarity of net returns to durable goods of all types including mines, in so doing he failed to encompass the long-standing debate as to whether mine income was rent or royalty by neglecting the question of the way in which the depreciation charge should be classified. Bohm-Bawerk's disregard for this 'rent or royalty' debate meant that it was then left to Gray to take up his methodology and give it particular significance in this context. As the next section will show, he did so by first arguing that Ricardo's contradictory treatment of mineral rents was the foundation for the debate.

The 'Rent or Royalty' Debate

Gray devotes considerable space to a resume of Ricardo's contradictory treatment of mineral rents and their status in relation to agricultural rents. He argues that the contemporaneous view that the return imputed to a mineral deposit consists of two parts (a rent and a royalty) is an attempt to harmonise the contradictory elements of Ricardo's analysis.[33]

Quoting Bohm-Bawerk's treatment of durable goods, Gray points out that for a durable good having an infinite productive life, the whole of the present income is regarded as interest, whereas income from a durable good having a finite productive life has two parts: firstly, a depreciation charge reflecting the fall in the value of the good which, when deducted from income leaves the second part which is regarded as interest.[34] Gray says that the first part - the depreciation charge - is what has been called a royalty while the second part - the interest - is what has been called rent.[35]

While there can be no objection, says Gray, to calling the depreciation charge a royalty, there is a problem with calling the residual income a rent. For, says Gray, every change in the rate of interest or in the 'degree of remoteness of exhaustibility' [sic] will change the amount of this so-called rent since it changes the amount of the so-called royalty.[36] The size of the so-called rent is thus 'not [solely] determined in amount by the conditions which give rise to a surplus over the expense of utilizing natural agents.'[37] That is, the so-called rent does not amount, as rent should, to the difference between revenue and extraction cost. Even when the difference between revenue and extraction cost remains unchanged, a change in the rate of interest or in the date on which the mine is exhausted will alter the value of the so-called royalty and thus the value of the so-called rent.[38] The 'true' rent is, in fact, the whole of the surplus over and above extraction cost. Nonetheless, says Gray, it remains that extraction of mineral today, rather than at some time in the future, involves a sacrifice of future surplus (a user cost). Should not the reward in the present which comes from making this sacrifice be construed as something other than 'true' rent? 'No', says Gray, for the sacrifice is simply a sacrifice of ['true'] rent itself which may have been earned at some other time. Gaffney puts it this way: '[Gray] is rejecting the notion of rent as a surplus of income above opportunity cost, where the foregone opportunity is simply another way of realizing some rent - in this case by withdrawing a mineral in the future instead of the present.'[39]

Gray thus concludes that although rent and royalty may be differentiated conceptually, they are one and the same thing - a surplus over extraction cost which should preferably be called 'rent' (or 'true rent'). He supports his argument by noting that Sorley recognised that rent and royalty are identical insofar as intramarginal mines are concerned[40]; and by this he presumably meant that Sorley did not identify a rent which was separate from the royalty but argued that differential mine rents are one and the same thing as the differential royalties paid to mine owners for the privilege of removing part of the contents of the mine. Gray's interpretation of Sorley's position in this respect is thus the same as the interpretation of Marshall which has been offered here in the previous chapter - an interpretation which Gray, himself, did not suggest.[41]

By showing that the whole of the mine surplus above extraction cost is rent, Gray had achieved the major task of his paper: 'to alter the Ricardian statement of rent in such a way as to avoid the necessity of assuming that rent is paid only for the "indestructible qualities of the soil".'[42] Although Gray offers no rigourous definition of the term 'rent', it would appear that he had in mind a definition which conforms to the old idea of rent as an unearned, price determined surplus over cost - where cost is Marshallian real cost rather than opportunity cost.[43]

In order to gain further evidence for the validity of his idea that the whole of the mine surplus is rent, Gray next considers whether confiscation of the surplus would be neutral. He suggests that although the so-called royalty could be confiscated in such a way as to affect production decisions and output prices, this outcome is in no way 'attributable to the fact that the royalty is capital which must be replaced.'[44] That is, the so-called royalty may also be confiscated in such a way as to be neutral; and this neutrality will be achieved if the method of confiscation has no effect on the relativity of returns from present and future. Indeed, confiscation of almost the whole of the mine surplus (so-called royalty plus so-called rent) can be neutral in its effect; and such a result may be achieved, for example, by levying a tax on the annual surplus of the mine.

This conclusion of Gray's is the aspect of his treatment of the economics of mineral extraction which has elicited most criticism. It has been argued that in concluding that confiscation of the surplus can be neutral, Gray has considered only its short run effects. He has not asked whether confiscation would be neutral in the long run; that is, whether it will affect the willingness to open new mines. Under certain restrictive assumptions, it can be shown that confiscation of the whole of the surplus may be neutral in the long run.[45] If, however, these restrictive assumptions do not apply and confiscation does affect long run supply, then at least part of what is confiscated cannot properly be called rent as Gray has done.

While Gray asserts that taxation involving careful confiscation of surplus may not alter short run production decisions, he does recognise that there are certain taxes which will not be neutral since they disturb the relationship between present and future. He considers two alternatives to the neutral tax. Firstly, he shows that an annual tax on the value of the mine will tilt the time-profile of production further towards the present, since shortening the life of the mine will reduce the total amount of tax paid; secondly, a unit tax will probably reduce the tilt towards the present since the effect of discounting the future tax is to decrease the net return of future production by less than the net return from present production is decreased.

Having used his consideration of the effects of taxation to reinforce his argument to the effect that the whole of the surplus of the mine is rent, Gray returns to the question of Ricardo's contradictory treatment of the rent of mines. He concludes that of the two solutions which Ricardo applied to the problem, the one in which he declared mineral rents to be determined in the same way as agricultural rents is the 'more nearly' correct explanation.[46] Gray says, however, that Ricardo was not correct in extending his theory of agricultural rent to the case of exhaustible resources. Such an extension requires, says Gray, modification of the proposition that production will be set at the level where product equals expense (where marginal revenue equals marginal cost); this modification being necessary on account of the competition between present and future uses which characterises resources of this type. Gray's paper concludes with a reassertion of the case for considering the whole of the surplus of the mine as rent:

'[T]he traditional division of the net return from exhaustible natural resources into a rent and a royalty is justified only as a method of capitalization. The real economic rent of such resources comprises the entire net return from the rent-bearer including the so-called royalty.'[47]

The surplus which Gray describes as the 'real economic rent' of the mine in the above statement is identical with the differential rent which Ricardo identified in that part of the *Principles* where he argued that mine rent is determined in the same way as agricultural rent. It is also identical with the differential royalty which Sorley identified and with the interpretation given above of Marshall's intramarginal royalty. Leaving aside the question of semantics (the question of whether 'rent' or 'royalty' is the appropriate term for this surplus), it is clear that, apart from introducing Bohm-Bawerk's neoclassical treatment of the mine into the context of the mineral economics literature, Gray has made no advance from the position of his predecessors insofar as the treatment of mine surplus is concerned. Indeed, in rejecting the idea that the marginal mine may normally yield a surplus, his treatment may be seen to be retrogressive in relation to that of his immediate predecessors - Sorley and Marshall.

On the other hand, that part of Gray's treatment of the nature of mine surplus which considers the effects of taxation on decision making in the mine represents an advance from the work of his predecessors and is of similar significance to his earlier treatment of the micro economics of the mine. This aspect is further considered in the conclusion.

Conclusion

It is clear that Gray's contribution to the development of the economics of exhaustible resources is of immense importance. Although Harold Hotelling is most often credited with creation of the seminal work in the modern theory of the economics of exhaustible resources, there can be no doubt that Gray's 1914 mineral economics paper is of similar significance in terms of its content - although Hotelling's more elegant paper is the one which is more often cited.

The greatest strength of Gray's mineral economics paper is its analysis of the decision making of the mine owner-operator which, in the context of the literature dealing with the economics of mineral extraction, represents a signal advance from the work of his predecessors. The greatest weakness of Gray's paper lies in his theory-dependent conclusion that the marginal mine will not, as a matter of course, yield a surplus over extraction cost. This conclusion represents a retreat from the position taken by his immediate predecessors and presents certain problems for an interpretation of his position regarding the user cost of mineral extraction - the final aspect of his paper to be assessed here.

The major significance of Gray's contribution to the literature lies in his recognition that the mine owner, in making production decisions, takes into account the user cost of production. This explanation of the importance of user cost was possible only because of his assumption that the mine has a capitalised value. Although Gray makes this assumption, the justification for it is not clear.

The assumption that the mine has a capitalised value might be taken to signify the existence of a regime of decreasing return on the extensive margin - for the implication of such a regime is that mines which are currently being worked will have a capitalised value reflecting their superiority, *cet. par.*, over mines to which resort must be had in the future when these existing mines are exhausted. A regime of decreasing return on the extensive margin is, however, also one in which, *cet. par.*, marginal mines have a capitalised value and in which output prices rise over time. Gray specifically argues that it is not possible for the marginal mine to have a capitalised value, and he also assumes constant output prices. That is, he allows that only intramarginal mines may have a capitalised value and assumes that they do so in an environment of constant output prices. Whether this assumption is one which is intended to reflect reality or whether it is simply operational is not clear. However, if it is taken to reflect reality, as Gray's cursory treatment of the possibility of rising prices suggests it should be, then the mineral industry which Gray analyses is one in which intramarginal mines have a capitalised value, marginal mines have no capitalised value and output prices remain constant over time. Although the existence of an industry having a concurrence of these three characteristics may seem unlikely in reality, these characteristics may be readily assimilated into a theoretical model.

The type of model which is consistent with these three characteristics is one in which, at any time, a number of operating mines - each having different extraction costs - forms a set of mines which will be replaced when simultaneous exhaustion occurs, by a new set of mines having identical costs. In other words, the model is one in which the short run industry supply curve is identical in every period although, as exhaustion occurs, the mines which make up the curve are periodically being replaced by similar mines. In such a model, the unchanging shape and position of the supply curve means, *cet. par.*, that: i) output price will remain constant over time; ii) the marginal mine will yield no surplus since it is not superior to those mines which will be marginal in the future; and, iii) at any time there will be intramarginal mines which will yield a surplus and have a capitalised value by virtue of their superiority over the present marginal mine.

Although it is impossible to determine from his mineral economics paper whether Gray had such a model in mind (or even in the back of his mind) - his statement of the prospects for the mineral industries which was made in his earlier conservation paper leaves the reader with no alternative but to conclude that he was not thinking of a model such as the one suggested here.

Speaking of the particular significance of the mineral industries Gray says:

> 'Minerals afford a tolerably clear-cut type of resources which are absolutely limited in supply and non-restorable. It is necessary to make a definite choice between present and future. Normally, when once used, the supply is exhausted practically for all time. The particular mine is poorer by reason of the extraction of its contents; and there is no reason for restoring to it from other sources the elements removed in the process of production. Not only is the particular mine poorer, but the entire potential supply of minerals is reduced by this utilization. ...[T]he most serious phases of the conservation problem grow out of the fact that some of the most important elements, such as coal, petroleum, and iron, are being rapidly and completely used up without hope of replacement.'[48]

This quotation suggests a view of the mineral industries which is consistent with a relatively high user cost of extraction associated with decreasing return on the extensive margin. This view, is, in turn, consistent with the emphasis which Gray gives in his mineral economics paper to the relevance of user cost for short run decision making in the mine. On the other hand, this emphasis on user cost remains in conflict with his negation of the idea that the marginal mine will earn a surplus and, if it was meant to be realistic, with his assumption of constant output price. As the next chapter will show, it was Gray's contemporary Gustav Cassel who was the first of the contributors to the mineral economics literature to successfully, if only partially, integrate changes on the extensive margin with events on the intensive margin.

Although no reconciliation of Gray's conflicting ideas is possible from available evidence, the general tenor of his contribution involves the maintenance of the pessimistic Ricardian emphasis on recourse to inferior resources; and this emphasis, is, of course, what might be expected of a literature which was contributed in the heyday of the first conservation movement and was dedicated to its cause.

Leaving aside the question of whether this pessimistic emphasis was warranted, it is clear that it is crucial to a micro economic treatment of the mine which stresses the importance of antagonism between present and future production; and it was Gray's perspicacious treatment of the mine owner's response to this antagonism which has been widely recognised as constituting his original contribution to the economics of exhaustible resources. Furthermore, the tenor of this contribution has, with few exceptions, been perpetuated in the literature to this day.

Notes

1. L.C. Gray, 'The economic possibilities of conservation', *Quarterly Journal of Economics*, vol. 27 (1913).

2. L.C. Gray, 'Rent under the assumption of exhaustibility', *Quarterly Journal of Economics*, vol. 28 (1914), reprinted in M. Gaffney (ed.), *Extractive Resources and Taxation* (University of Wisconsin Press, Madison, 1967).

3. E.V. Bohm-Bawerk, *The Positive Theory of Capital*, translated by W. Smart (Books for Libraries Press, New York, 1971).

4. Although Bohm-Bawerk favoured a theoretical bipartite division of the factors of production, he argued for the continuation of the practical application of the existing tripartite division. See Bohm-Bawerk, *Positive Theory*, p. 357 *n*.

5. Ibid., pp. 354-7.

6. Ibid., bk VI, ch. VII-VIII.

7. Ibid., p. xiii.

8. G.J. Stigler, *The Theory of Price* (Macmillan, New York, 1950), p. 334.

9. H. Hotelling, 'The economics of exhaustible resources', *Journal of Political Economy*, vol. 39, no. 2 (1931).

10. Gray, 'Rent under the assumption of exhaustibility', pp. 423-4.

11. Ibid., pp. 424-6. It has been argued in the chapter above that, in distinguishing rent from royalty, Marshall had already made this point.

12. Sorley puts the argument the other way around. He says that a decision to extract mineral today means foregoing the possibility of future benefit.

13. A definition of positive price expectations can be found in J.R. Hicks, *Value and Capital*, 2nd edn (Oxford University Press, Oxford, 1946), p. 205. Gray did not use the term himself.

14. Gray, 1914, 'Rent under the assumption of exhaustibility', pp. 427-8.

15. Gray, 'The economic possibilities of conservation', pp. 504-5.

16. Gray, 'Rent under the assumption of exhaustibility', pp. 433-4. Gray also makes the tacit assumptions that the mining firm is a price taker and that the standard assumptions of short run production theory apply.

17. Ibid. Throughout his work Gray introduces relevant institutional factors which are often ignored by less careful analysts. The pitfalls of inappropriate assumptions about the nature of tenure systems are addressed by Fitzgibbons and Cochrane. A. Fitzgibbons and S. Cochrane, 'Optimal rate of natural resource depletion', *Resources Policy*, vol. 4, no. 3 (1978).

18. Gray, 'Rent under the assumption of exhaustibility', p. 429. In line with accepted convention, Gray takes the *in situ* mineral deposit as the short run fixed factor. Thus minimum unit cost will be determined on the basis of both capital and labour inputs being variable.

19. Ibid., table 1. Gray had already made this point in his conservation paper. Gray, 'The economic possibilities of conservation', p. 506.

20. Gray, 'Rent under the assumption of exhaustibility', table 2.

21. Gray, 'The economic possibilities of conservation', p. 506.

22. Gray, 'Rent under the assumption of exhaustibility', pp. 433-4.

23. Ibid., pp. 434-7, tables 3 and 4.

24. Ibid., p. 437.

25. Levhari and Liviatan have shown that a similar conclusion can be drawn if, *cet. par.*, the mine experiences rising extraction costs with cumulative production. They did not, however, consider the similar case of falling output prices, *cet. par.* D. Levhari and N. Liviatan, 'Notes on Hotelling's economics of exhaustible resources', *Canadian Journal of Economics*, vol. 10, no. 2 (1977).

26. He had already done so in his conservation paper. Gray, 'The economic possibilities of conservation', p. 505.

27. Gray, 'Rent under the assumption of exhaustibility', p. 431.

28. J.S. Mill had earlier suggested the existence of short run diminishing return but only in the case of some mines.

29. Gray, 'Rent under the assumption of exhaustibility', p. 437.

30. Ibid., p. 438. This is a classic example of a theory-dependent observation. See A.F. Chalmers, *What Is This Thing Called Science?*, 2nd edn (University of Queensland Press, St. Lucia, 1982), ch. 3.

31. Gray, 'Rent under the assumption of exhaustibility', p. 438.

32. In attributing to Sorley an explanation of the surplus or royalty on the margin which involves compensation to the mine owner for negative externalities associated with production, Gray misses Sorley's point entirely. Although Sorley does argue that exploitation of the marginal mine will 'not contribute to the amenity of the neighbourhood' and that a mine owner's decision to leave it unworked will 'preserve the beauty of his neighbourhood', the major reason which Sorley gives for the payment of a surplus to the owner of the marginal mine is that, unlike the marginal farm, the marginal mine deteriorates by being worked: 'Hence as mines deteriorate by being worked, the landlord will only let them at a rent bearing some proportion to the amount of deterioration they suffer. Even the least fertile mine worked will pay a rent of this kind, and this rent will enter into the price of the product.' W.R. Sorley, 'Mining royalties and their effect on the iron and coal trades', *Royal Statistical Society Journal*, vol. 52 (1889), p. 76. Gray's argument to the effect that Sorley explained the marginal mine's surplus as compensation for negative externalities can be found in Gray, 'Rent under the assumption of exhaustibility', p. 438 *n*.

33. Ibid., p. 438-40. Gray gives no evidence to support this claim and none has been found by the writer.

34. In this case, interest on the capitalised value of the mine. See Bohm-Bawerk, *Positive Theory*, bk VI, chapters VII-VIII.

35. Again, Gray gives no evidence for this assertion and none has been found by the writer. It was Marshall who specifically stated that mine income is partly rent and partly royalty, and Gray may have had Marshall in mind when making this point. A comparison of Gray's treatment of mining with Marshall's has been undertaken by Henry Steele. However, his objective was different from that being pursued here and his interpretation of Marshall's position is largely conjectural. See H. Steele, 'Natural resource taxation: resource allocation and distribution implications' in Gaffney, *Extractive Resources*, pp. 235-9.

36. Gray, 'Rent under the assumption of exhaustibility', p. 441.

37. Ibid.

38. Gray's partial analysis tacitly involves the idea that the rate of interest is given to the mining sector by the rest of the economy. Some of the implications of a mining sector which has a significant role in determining the rate of interest are considered by Fitzgibbons and Cochrane. A. Fitzgibbons, 'Optimal rate of natural resource depletion', pp. 166-8.

39. Gaffney, *Extractive Resources*, p. 4.

40. Gray, 'Rent under the assumption of exhaustibility', p. 441 *n*.

41. If Gray believed that Marshall's division of surplus into rent and royalty implied Bohm-Bawerk's interest and depreciation charge respectively, it is not surprising that he did not rely on Marshall for support. The view that Marshall was not implying a division of surplus such as Bohm-Bawerk suggested is reinforced by Cassel's opinion that since mine surplus is partly depreciation and partly interest, the distinction which Marshall made between rent and royalty cannot be sustained. G. Cassel, *The Theory of Social Economy*, translated by J. McCabe (Fisher Unwin, London, 1923), p. 280 *n*.

42. Gray, 'Rent under the assumption of exhaustibility', pp. 425-6.

43. See J.A. Schumpeter, *History of Economic Analysis* (George Allen and Unwin, London, 1954), pp. 936-7.

44. Gray, 'Rent under the assumption of exhaustibility', p. 443.

45. These assumptions would include the absence of exploration cost and perfect knowledge of the nature and extent of newly discovered deposits. See Steele, 'Natural resource taxation', pp. 238-9.

46. Gray, 'Rent under the assumption of exhaustibility', p. 445.

47. Ibid., p. 446. What Gray here describes as the 'net' return is identical with Bohm-Bawerk's 'gross' return.

48. Gray, 'The economic possibilities of conservation', pp. 501-2.

13

Gustav Cassel

Cassel's *Theory of Social Economy* which contains a thorough discussion of the economics of mineral extraction was first published in German in 1918 - an English translation being first published in 1923.[1] In his preface to the first edition Cassel explains that his manuscript was prepared by 1914 when the outbreak of war prevented publication. This is the same year in which Gray's paper 'Rent Under the Assumption of Exhaustibility' was published and it seems that the conclusions reached by Cassel - many of which were similar to Gray's - were achieved independently of Gray's work.

Whereas Gray's work and the later contribution of Hotelling were both presented in article form, Cassel's analysis of mining constituted but a small part of a more general treatment of the principles of economics; and this format may help to explain why Cassel's contribution has been ignored by both contemporaneous and more recent authors. On the other hand, Cassel was internationally famous at the height of his career in the 1920s and it is surprising that at this time his analysis of the economics of mineral extraction was not assimilated into the small literature dealing with the subject.[2] Certainly, Cassel's contribution is of great merit and whatever the reasons for its neglect, they cannot relate to the inherent quality of his work.

As this chapter will show, Cassel's contribution is at least the equal of Gray's. Cassel draws many of the original conclusions also drawn by Gray, makes some significant advances in relation to Gray's work and gives, on the whole, a superior treatment of mine surplus to that given by Gray. In short, Cassel offers a wide ranging treatment of the economics of mineral extraction which is

157

thoroughly neoclassical and which is a fitting precursor to Hotelling's later definitive treatment.[3]

This chapter commences with a brief discussion of Cassel's analysis of the general nature of rent - an analysis which he used as the background for a separate discussion of the nature of the rent of mines. This discussion of the rent of mines is the next aspect of Cassel's work to be reviewed in this chapter and it precedes an appraisal of his extensive treatment of decision making in the mine and the effects of changes in the values of relevant variables upon it. The interrelationship between different mines in the context of a mineral industry is the next aspect of Cassel's work to be discussed here and this constitutes the last aspect of his treatment of mineral extraction to be reviewed. Maintaining the format of previous chapters, the final aspect of Cassel's work to be discussed is his position regarding Carey's argument for increasing return on the extensive margin of cultivation. The chapter then closes with some concluding remarks.

The Nature of Rent

In discussing the nature of rent, Cassel had two major objectives. Firstly, he was concerned to give the subject of rent a thoroughly neoclassical treatment by perpetuating the already established view - associated with Bohm-Bawerk and others - that it relates to returns from durable goods of all kinds including those which occur in nature and those which are man-made. Secondly, he wished to establish that the returns to natural agents other than indestructible land were, at least in part, not rent. In this latter aspect, it will be shown that Cassel's approach differs significantly from Gray's and, unlike Gray's contribution, represents a logical refinement of the work of Sorley and Marshall.

Following Ricardo, Cassel argues that *rent proper* as he calls it is 'the price of the use of the original and indestructible forces of the land.'[4] Its existence 'is determined simply by the necessity of restricting the demand for the scarce use of the land.'[5] Rent, says Cassel, cannot be regarded as remuneration for any productive activity - regardless of whether that activity is directed towards the creation of new goods or the maintenance of old. That is, in order to determine the *rent proper* of land, both the returns to its man-made features and the returns which bring with them the necessity for reinstatement of original features must be excluded from the gross return.[6]

However, in certain cases part of the returns to man-made durable goods is, according to Cassel, of the nature of *rent* although it is not *rent proper* as he has defined it.[7] This being the case, the term *rent* may, in general usage, be defined as 'the price of the use of a durable good.'[8] But this means, says Cassel, that 'a price paid for consumable goods is not a rent, even when the articles are what we call free natural goods.'[9] Thus incomes derived from the sale of mineral products or timber from virgin forests are not *rents proper* nor are they *rents*; although practically speaking they are very similar to *rents* if they are realised over very long periods of time.[10]

Cassel argues that logic demands that such outputs as minerals or timber from virgin forests must be regarded as factors of production distinct and separate from land (meaning the original and indestructible features of land). He uses the term *natural materials* to describe these distinct and separate factors, advocating that they be given separate consideration from the other natural factor which he continues to describe as *land*.[11] Cassel's position in this regard maintains and formalises a tradition which had its roots in Ricardo's distinction between the different bases for 'rent' in agriculture and in mining (or forestry) and which was maintained and further developed by both Sorley and Marshall. It is a position which is, however, contrary to that taken by Gray who argued that the whole of mine surplus is rent. The differences between Cassel and Gray in this respect are further considered in the next section.

The Rent of Mines

On the basis of his emphasis on the need for a distinctly different treatment of *natural materials* as compared to *land*, Cassel devotes a separate section of his overall treatment of the returns from natural resources to their case - indeed, the chapter which deals with the nature of returns to natural resources is called 'Ground Rents and the Prices of Natural Materials'. In his discussion of natural materials, Cassel chooses to consider only one example from this class, namely, minerals.

In discussing the return to natural materials Cassel again asserts that their price is simply the price of consumption goods found in nature. If materials such as coal or ore are extracted and delivered to consumers, their prices consist mainly of payment for the services of capital and labour which are used to extract and transport them. Although only a small part of their price is payment for the *in situ* mineral it is this part which is the subject of Cassel's analysis.[12] The idea that only a small part of the value of the mineral output is payment for the *in situ* mineral itself may be taken to imply a relatively low user cost of exploitation; and this clue as to Cassel's position regarding the user cost of mineral extraction will be taken up again in the conclusion to this chapter.

Noting that the total stock of mineral in a mine cannot be exploited immediately but must be extracted over a fairly long time period, Cassel explains that the value of the total *in situ* stock of a mineral is equal to the present value of the future stream of returns. The annual return from the mine will thus be partly interest on this capitalised value and partly a depreciation charge.[13] In the early years of a mine's life the greater part of the return will be interest while in the later years the greater part will be depreciation. In the case of a mine having a very long life, the value of the *in situ* material mined annually is thus essentially in the nature of interest on the capitalised value of the mine and is akin to the price paid for use of a durable good; that is, akin to a rent.[14] This, says Cassel, explains why the income which a mine owner receives by virtue of his ownership of free gifts of nature is often regarded as a rent similar to the income received by a landlord.[15] This analysis of the nature of the income from a mine is one in which only the interest on the value of the mine is classed as rent or akin to rent and it is essentially the same analysis as was presented by Bohm-Bawerk. However, it is, as earlier noted, at variance with Gray's opinion that the whole of the income of the mine (both interest and depreciation charge) is rent.

Having illustrated the general nature of income from the mine, Cassel continues his analysis of mining with a wide-ranging discussion of those factors which relate to the determination of this income.

The Economics of Mining

Declaring that his analysis is confined to the conditions of an exchange economy, Cassel says that, in general, the prices of *in situ* natural materials are determined by the general pricing process and are scarcity prices which serve the purpose of limiting demand. On the basis of an assumption that constant output prices prevail, Cassel proceeds to a partial analysis of the pricing process as it relates to the contents of the individual mine.

In the individual mine, the owner-operator is, says Cassel, faced with a trade off which involves the realisation that while an increase in the present value of the mine may be achieved by shortening the period over which its finite contents are won, at the same time, this shortening of the period increases the total cost of extracting these contents. It is clear that unlike Marshall but like Gray, Cassel believed that short run diminishing return is experienced in the mine.[16]

Explaining that the owner-operator must make the best of the trade off between present and future production, Cassel points out that he may do so by reducing all income and expenditure over the life of the mine to their present values. If, for example, an increase in the rate of production which increases the present value of capital and labour costs produces an even greater increase in the present value of sales revenue then it is advantageous to bring production forward in time.[17] Although Cassel would not have used the term, he is clearly arguing that marginal analysis will enable the owner-operator to maximise return:

> 'Hence the mine-owner must, during the period of working, invest in his business so much capital that the final increase of the present value of the cost of labour and capital is outweighed by the final increase of the present value of the total sales which it secures.'[18]

Although Cassel's treatment of decision making in the mine is much more succinct than is Gray's, like Gray's work it involves the problem of maximising return from a finite *in situ* deposit having a capitalised value. However, in his more neoclassical approach, Cassel, unlike Gray, does not pursue the theme of differences between decision making in the mine and on the farm. Neither does he allude to the tilt towards the present in the time profile of production which Gray had mentioned - although the idea of the tilt is implicit in his later discussion of the effects of changes in the discount rate. Cassel continues his discussion of optimisation in the mine by considering in turn the effects of a change in the price of the mineral output, the effects of a change in the rate of interest and the effects of uncertainty.

A once and for all increase in the current and expected price of the mineral output will, says Cassel, increase the advantage of production in the present, *cet. par.;* thus shortening the life of the mine. Again, this conclusion is identical to Gray's. However, Cassel adds another dimension to the analysis of the effects of price changes by next considering the relevance of expected future prices for the determination of current price.

The needs of the future are guaranteed, says Cassel, by the fact that in an exchange economy based on private enterprise an expected future scarcity resulting from resource depletion will result in higher expected future prices which will have the effect, *cet. par.*, of reducing current production. This reduced current production will, *cet. par.*, increase current prices and rather than prices remaining constant for a time and then showing a significant rise consequent upon the depletion induced future scarcity, they will tend to rise at a more uniform rate. That is, current prices reflect future scarcity.[19] This particular link between the present and the future is here presented explicitly for the first time in the literature dealing with the economics of mineral extraction; and not only is it an aspect ignored by Cassel's predecessors but in suggesting that future scarcity involves a more or less uniform rise in price over time it also anticipates Hotelling's later treatment.[20] As the concluding remarks to this chapter will indicate, this finding of Cassel's is also significant because, for the first time in the mineral economics literature, the nature of the extensive margin is explicitly and satisfactorily integrated with the treatment of decision making on the intensive margin.[21] Having considered the effects of price changes, Cassel next turns to the relevance of the rate of interest and of uncertainty for decision making in the mine.

An increase in the rate of interest will, says Cassel, tilt the existing time profile of production towards the present since, *cet. par.*, it decreases the present value of future production.[22] Although Cassel nowhere mentions whether the existing time profile of production involves a tilt as Gray had suggested, its existence is, as earlier remarked, implicit in his treatment of a rise in the discount rate and can easily be verified by considering the effect of a rise in the rate from zero to some positive level.

Not only do changes in prices and interest rates affect production decisions but the factor of uncertainty also plays an important role. The existence of uncertainty is considered by Cassel to favour present over future production, *cet. par.* He cites the possibility of new discoveries and the progress of technology in the area of the development of substitutes for mineral output as well as improvements in production processes as reasons for mine owners to bring production forward in time.[23] This treatment of uncertainty which introduces factors evocative of the optimism of both Adam Smith and Carey is an aspect of mineral extraction that is absent from Gray's work - and this absence is not surprising in view of the pessimistic conservationist stance which he took.

Having considered the effects of changes in the values of key variables upon decision making in the mine, Cassel briefly considers the relevance of market imperfections. In a manner suggestive of Hotelling's later and more rigorous treatment Cassel first considers the effect of monopolistic control over a natural material. He offers the novel, yet intuitively reasonable argument that monopoly control restricts present consumption and 'tends to secure more regard for the wants of the future.'[24] State intervention is another important aspect leading to market imperfections and Cassel notes that intervention by way of export embargoes and taxes is not uncommon and that it increases current global scarcity of natural materials thus better serving the interests of the future.[25] Explaining that the values of natural materials depend as much on the nature of the industry in which the firm operates as they do on the nature of the firm itself, Cassel concludes his discussion of the latter and turns to the former.

The Mineral Industry

Cassel commences his discussion of the relevance of the nature of the industry in which the mining firm operates by first considering an industry comprising just two firms - each exploiting a single mine. He notes that although these mines may have different costs, their output will sell at the same price at the place of consumption.[26] If certain (unspecified) conditions prevail, says Cassel, it is possible for market price to be such as to give the *in situ* mineral at both the lower and higher cost mines a capitalised value. There is no suggestion from Cassel that the surplus of the higher cost mine which gives rise to its capitalised value is one which might be expected as a matter of course and it is likely that Cassel was thinking of cases such as Ricardo and Mill had suggested where indivisibilities explain the existence of the surplus.

This interpretation is supported by the next stage of Cassel's industry analysis in which he considers an industry consisting of a large number of mines. If, he says, market price is such that the 'last' or marginal mine covers only labour and capital costs then the value of the *in situ* mineral in that mine will be zero. The values of the contents of all other mines will then reflect the difference between their capital and labour costs and those of the marginal mine. If one follows the old theory of rent, says Cassel, this means that the value of the *in situ* mineral does not enter into price. Cassel argues that although this proposition is formally correct, it, nonetheless, distorts the pricing process in the same way as does the traditional theory of (agricultural) rent. For, the surplus of the mine is not price determined but is, like agricultural rent, determined simultaneously with all other relevant values.[27] It can be inferred from this analysis of a mineral industry comprising a number of mines that Cassel believed that, with perfect divisibility, the marginal mine would not earn a surplus as a matter of course. This inference may be tested by examining his treatment of the extensive margin in which the long run effects of a rise in price are considered.

Cassel first notes the effects of an increase in price associated with high demand occurring at the peak of the trade cycle. Assuming a time period short enough to preclude significant technological change, he says that these circumstances will involve more intensive working of existing mines, the reopening of previously idle mines, and the establishment of new, higher cost mines.[28] The last of these occurrences involves the need for resort to inferior resources and although Cassel did not mention the possibility, could thus be interpreted as being consistent with the idea that the mine on the extensive margin will typically yield a surplus (pay a royalty to its owner). This interpretation may, however, be inconsistent with Cassel's view of the role of technological change in mining. Once technological change is accounted for, says Cassel, the long run elasticity of supply of minerals will be found to be relatively high. He cites improvements in mining techniques, in transport and in processing as well as the great abundance of poor ores as reasons for a relatively high elasticity.[29] Clearly each of these factors could promote extension of the margin to superior resources (changes in the ranking of deposits) which would preclude the existence of a surplus on the extensive margin. Indeed, in the concluding remarks to his chapter dealing with rent and the prices of raw materials Cassel leaves his reader on a highly optimistic note. Discussing technological change which has enabled the economical use of lower quality ores he states that it 'is obvious how very important all these advances are as regards the supply of natural materials to civilised man. Of poor ores - of materials of poor quality generally - nature has, as a rule, a great abundance'.[30] The similarity of this optimism to the optimism which Cassel displays in relation to agriculture is taken up in the next section.

Extension of the Agricultural Margin

The first point which Cassel makes and for which his logic is impeccable is that, *cet. par.*, agricultural extension at any particular time will involve the use of land having higher costs of production than land already in use. If this were not so then farmers would prefer to switch cultivation to the unused land rather than continue cultivating some or all of the land already in use.[31] Cassel goes on to argue, however, that under certain circumstances all other factors do not remain constant and extension of the margin of cultivation may involve the inclusion of new lands having costs no greater than (and, indeed, possibly lower than) those of existing marginal land.

One of the circumstances conducive to this outcome is a fall in capital costs associated with the development of new arable lands requiring capital intensive techniques for this development. Such a circumstance is, says Cassel, what one might expect in a country in its early years of colonisation. Interest rates in such a country may be expected to be relatively high initially, thus favouring less capital intensive techniques for the development of arable land. If, at a later stage, interest rates are significantly lower, then more capital intensive land development techniques may be employed and may result in the development of lands having no greater cultivation cost than those already in use.[32] Although Cassel makes no mention of Carey in putting forward this hypothesis, it is clearly evocative of his work.

Technological advance relating to agricultural methods is another circumstance which Cassel says may lead to previously unused land being cultivated at no greater cost than land already in use. However, no matter what the cause, it is clear that the rank order of agricultural lands according to their output costs is likely to change over time:

'It cannot, therefore, be taken for granted that different areas of land were drawn into cultivation in the sequence which would correspond to the degree of quality assigned to them under the present conditions of technical knowledge and social organization.'[33]

Although Cassel is here considering only the case of agriculture, it is clear that he concurs with Carey's optimistic conclusion; and, furthermore, his extensive discussion of increasing return in agriculture is in similar vein to his brief consideration of this possibility in mining.

Conclusion

Cassel's contribution to the literature of the economics of mineral extraction is of similar significance to that of Lewis Gray, although Cassel's treatment is much more succinct. It is, however, a contribution which has not been recognised in the recent literature and it was certainly not acknowledged as a source of inspiration in the contemporaneous literature. Furthermore, as mentioned in the introductory remarks to this chapter, it is a contribution which originated independently of, but at much the same time as, Gray's work.

On the basis of this last observation it would be difficult to over emphasise the importance of Cassel's contribution to the development of the economics of mineral extraction. Compared to the work of late nineteenth century authors such as Sorley and Marshall, Cassel's contribution constituted a highly significant advance. An advance which might reasonably be argued to involve a more successful integration of the economics of mining into the context of a neoclassical framework than the attempts of any of his predecessors - including Gray.

Although Cassel's treatment of the micro economics of mining is not as detailed as Gray's, nonetheless, like Gray's work it establishes the importance of marginal adjustment of the time profile of production and successfully considers the effects of factors such as changes in output price, changes in interest rates, and expectations.

It is in relation to this last aspect that Cassel makes a significant and novel contribution which involves the secular trend of price and which had eluded Gray who assumed constant output prices. This novel contribution contains the idea that expected future scarcity affects current prices and that it does so in such a way as to promote a steady rise in price over time. Thus, not only did Cassel successfully analyse the intensive margin of production but he was also successful in integrating changes on the extensive margin with behaviour on the intensive margin - at least in the case where extension of the margin involves a depletion induced resort to inferior resources. The question of whether or not it can be inferred from this significant finding that Cassel considered cases of decreasing return on the extensive margin to be common is an important one and it will be addressed later in this conclusion. At this stage, however, it is conclusions about Cassel's treatment of mine surplus which will be addressed.

Cassel offers no systematic explanation for the existence of mine surplus - save to say that it derives from a scarcity price which reflects the need to limit demand and that it may be measured by the 'old' differential principle. He does, however, present an analysis of its nature which is thoroughly neoclassical and which is unlike Gray's analysis in that it maintains the tradition of treating at least part of the income of the mine as something other than rent. Just as Gray had done, Cassel integrated a Bohm-Bawerkian approach to income from exhaustible resources into the context of the literature of the economics of mineral extraction. In so doing he has, unlike Gray, maintained the distinction between rent and royalty by deducting the component of surplus which represents the depreciation charge or royalty from the gross surplus to give a net surplus which he describes as rent.

Whether the whole of the gross surplus over extraction cost should be called rent as Gray has done or whether it is only the net surplus which should be so called is, in many respects, a question of semantics. However, in taking the latter position Cassel avoids many of the problems which later critics of Gray suggested were associated with a position which treated the whole of the surplus as rent. In particular, to treat the royalty or depreciation charge as something other than rent, as Cassel has done, is to emphasise the opportunity cost of depletion. In the remaining part of this conclusion an assessment of Cassel's idea of the extent of user cost involved in mineral extraction will be undertaken.

Cassel provides a number of clues as to the significance of user cost. Those clues which suggest that user cost is relatively low or zero are three in number. Firstly, in discussing mineral output prices Cassel declares that only a small part of the price is payment for the *in situ* mineral; secondly, he nowhere specifically suggests that with perfect divisibility of the production unit there will be a surplus on the extensive margin; and, thirdly, he suggests that as a result, *inter alia*, of the development of transport and of techniques for the use of highly abundant inferior ores, the long term elasticity of supply of minerals is relatively high. Now, each of these three factors is clearly consistent with the others and each points to a relatively insignificant role for user cost. On the other hand, it is implicit in Cassel's analysis of optimising behaviour of the mine owner that present and future production are antagonistic and that present production therefore involves a positive user cost. The idea that there are intramarginal mines which will yield a surplus may also be taken to imply positive user cost - as may his discussion of the likelihood of rises in present prices consequent upon an expectation of future scarcity.

Clearly, no definitive conclusion can be drawn as to the overall importance which Cassel placed on user cost. However, in the context of the development of the economics of mineral extraction, his reliance on the role of user cost in his analysis of short run decision making by the mine owner may be seen as one of the earliest examples of a tradition which is perpetuated in the literature today. On the other hand, those aspects of his analysis from which it might be inferred that mineral extraction has a low user cost are aspects which are given less prominence in the modern theoretical literature.

Finally, Cassel's wide ranging discussion of various aspects of mineral extraction might simply be interpreted as involving an approach which allows the possibility of either high or low user cost depending, *inter alia*, on the nature of the mineral industry under scrutiny and on the stage of its historical development.

Notes

1. G. Cassel, *The Theory of Social Economy*, translated by J. McCabe (Fisher Unwin, London, 1923). A second edition translated by S.L. Barron was published in English in 1932. Its treatment of the subject matter to be discussed in this chapter is virtually identical with that of the first edition which is relied on almost exclusively in the assessment of Cassel which follows.

2. On Cassel's stature in the 1920s see J.A. Schumpeter, *History of Economic Analysis* (George, Allen and Unwin, London, 1954), p. 1154 *n*.

3. H. Hotelling, 'The economics of exhaustible resources', *Journal of Political Economy*, vol. 39, no. 2, (1931).

4. Cassel, *Theory*, p. 257.

5. Ibid.

6. Ibid.

7. Ibid., pp. 260-1. Cassel has in mind certain existing man-made capital goods which have a uniqueness relating either to the fact that they are no longer produced or to the fact that significant changes have occurred in their production cost.

8. Ibid., p. 256.

9. Ibid.

10. Ibid.

11. Ibid. Although Cassel followed Bohm-Bawerk in arguing that the returns to durable goods of all types are explained in the same way, like Bohm-Bawerk he found it fruitful to divide these goods into different classes. However, rather than maintain the tripartite division of factors of production as Bohm-Bawerk had done he argued for a four part division - adding *natural materials* to the conventional trio.

12. Ibid., pp. 279-80.

13. Ibid., p. 280. This conclusion is identical with Bohm-Bawerk's and with Gray's. Although Cassel's translators used the term 'sinking fund' rather than the term 'depreciation charge', the latter term was used by Gray and will be used in this chapter to maintain continuity with the previous chapter. At no stage does Cassel explain the conditions which give rise to the *in situ* mineral having a capitalised value. However, as will be seen shortly, he later offers a clue when he explains how changes in this value might come about.

14. Ibid.

15. Ibid.

16. Although the idea of short run diminishing return is implicit in Cassel's assertion that a higher rate of extraction involves a higher total cost of extraction of the contents of the mine, nowhere does he explicitly mention the nature of short run return in the mine. He had, however, earlier argued that diminishing return is relevant to every branch of production. See ibid., p. 269. It is interesting that in considering changes in the rate of extraction of the whole of the contents of the mine, Cassel, like Marshall, avoided the problems associated with the return to cumulative extraction.

17. Cassel, *Theory*, p. 282.

18. Ibid.

19. Ibid., p. 283. In explaining how prices rise consequent upon an expected future scarcity, Cassel provides a clue as to the source of the capitalised value which he earlier assumed was characteristic of the *in situ* mineral.

20. Hotelling, 'The economics of exhaustible resources', pp. 140-1.

21. Sorley came close to this integration when he suggested that since the mine is a potential source of income in the future, its owner would rather see it lie idle than have it worked without receiving some compensation.

22. Cassel, *Theory*, p. 283.

23. Ibid.

24. Ibid., p. 284. Whether this argument is, in fact, correct has been a contentious issue in the recent literature. See F.M. Peterson and A.C. Fisher, 'The exploitation of extractive resources a survey', *Economic Journal*, vol. 87 (1977), pp. 694-5, and A.L. Hillman and N.V. Long, 'Substitutes for a depletable resource and the monopolistic conservationist presumption', *Australian Economic Papers*, vol. 21, no. 38 (1982).

25. Cassel, *Theory*, p. 285. Consistent with his treatment of other aspects of the economy, Cassel also considers the rate of exploitation of natural materials in a socialist state. He argues that an isolated socialist society can choose what it considers to be an appropriate rate of exploitation with hardly any regard to the rate of interest. Ibid., p. 284.

26. Ibid., p. 285.

27. Ibid., pp. 285-6. It is here, and in this context, that Cassel criticised Marshall's contention that mineral royalties enter into price whereas agricultural rents do not.

28. Ibid., pp. 286-7.

29. Ibid., p. 287.

30. Ibid.

31. Ibid., p. 275.

32. Ibid., p. 275-6.

33. This quotation is from the second edition (1932). The same point is made in a somewhat ambiguous way in the first edition and the wording of the second has been used here to avoid that ambiguity. See G. Cassel, *The Theory of Social Economy*, 2nd edn (Harcourt, Brace, New York, 1932), p. 286, and Cassel, *Theory*, 1st edn, p. 276.

14
Conclusion

With the possible exceptions of Henry Carey and Karl Marx each
of the authors whose work has been reviewed in this study made
a significant contribution to the development of the mainstream
theoretical treatment of the economics of exhaustible resources. It
is clear that although Hotelling's 1931 paper is considered to be
the seminal work in the field, the literature produced in the one
hundred and fifty years prior to the publication of that paper is a
rich source of foundation material. In particular, the contributions
made by Sorley and those who followed him gave distinct emphasis
to the notion of present production from the mine involving an
intertemporal opportunity cost - a user cost. These contributions
thus embodied an idea which is central to the later neoclassical
treatment of the subject. Although there was agreement that mine
production might involve a user cost, there remained some
unresolved or unsatisfactorily treated matters. The most important
of these were the question of the way in which the income of the
mine should be classified, and the nature of return on the
extensive margin of production. With regard to this latter aspect,
the contributors to the literature generally failed to integrate the
idea of mine production involving a user cost with an appropriate
picture of the way in which the extensive margin shifts out over
time. In particular, many of the authors who emphasised the idea
that production from the mine involves a user cost also suggested
that an historical progression to superior *in situ* mineral resources
might be as likely an occurrence as is resort to inferior resources.
This failure to integrate the nature of the intensive margin with the
dynamics of the extensive margin is also made manifest in the
literature by the unresolved argument as to whether the marginal
mine will yield a 'surplus'. Not only were the shortcomings of the

literature related to a failure to recognise the significance of the nature of return on the extensive margin for mineral values but, in this aspect and in many others, they were also related to inappropriate application of the static, differential theory of agricultural rent to mines.

Contrasting views about the nature of return on the extensive margin have been given particular emphasis throughout this study. It has been shown that although Ricardo was responsible for the essentially pessimistic view upon which the neoclassical theory is based, Adam Smith, Carey and Marx displayed a great degree of optimism. In this respect Carey's contribution is of particular significance since he argued that in some industries extension of the margin of production may involve a *systematic* progression to superior resources. While Smith, Carey and Marx gave particular emphasis to the optimistic idea of the extensive margin being characterised by increasing return, this was a possibility which was seriously entertained by almost all of the authors whose work has been reviewed here. In spite of repeated mention of this possibility, the one hundred and fifty years of research into the economics of exhaustible resources which has been reviewed here culminated in an essentially pessimistic treatment of the topic which emphasised the role of user cost in determination of the optimal time profile of production from the finite contents of the mine - a treatment which thus emphasised the so-called 'cake eating' problem. This emphasis upon user cost was particularly apparent in Gray's work and, notwithstanding Cassel's optimism, in the later work of Hotelling. It is also a feature of the extensive literature dealing with exhaustible resources which has been produced in the recent past. While the culmination of one and a half centuries of analysis of mining involved a model which implies, but seldom explicitly mentions, a regime of decreasing return on the extensive margin of production, the outcome of the analysis of agriculture over the same period was very different. Although Henry Carey had suggested that increasing return on the extensive margin might characterise both mining and agriculture, it was only in the case of agriculture that his arguments for increasing return were taken up by later authors; and, as the reviews of the works of Carey, Mill, Marx and Marshall have indicated, by the end of the nineteenth century there was ready acceptance of these arguments in the mainstream literature.

It is clear from their writings that both Lewis Gray and Harold Hotelling were greatly influenced by the first conservation movement and in the period from approximately 1890 to 1930 a considerable pessimistic literature was produced - particularly in the United States. At the same time as this literature appeared a number of authors noted the optimistic possibility of increasing return on the extensive margin in mining and some of them gave practical examples of such a regime. Furthermore, these authors discussed this possibility in the context of new countries and old. In this regard, L.H. Courtney's discussion of the abandoning of copper and tin mines in Cornwall at the turn of the century is relevant. These events which were the result of competition from new, low cost mines on the extensive margin abroad were mentioned in Chapter 3. A graphic example of the importance of increasing return on the extensive margin had earlier been given by the Duke of Argyll - an economic commentator of some note who was a mine owner himself.[1] In defence of Adam Smith's argument that the least cost mine has a role in regulating price, the Duke discussed his own experiences in the nickel mining industry.[2]

In the 1860s nickel was found on the Duke's property in Scotland and a profitable mining exercise was commenced. Shortly thereafter, the opening of a Norwegian mine containing easily accessible but lower grade ore resulted in a diminution of market price. The Duke continued to operate his mine - although less profitably - until the discovery of cheaper and more abundant supplies, especially those of the Pacific islands, reduced the market price of nickel to such an extent that he was forced to abandon his mine:

'The produce of those cheaper machines "regulated" the only price which I could get for the produce of my poorer machine, until at a certain point of this "regulating" process, my mine was regulated out of its existence altogether. The price of nickel was regulated down to so low a point that my poorer and more expensive mine became no longer worth working.'[3]

Increasing return on the extensive margin resulted in the Duke abandoning his mine; and, from the limited information he has given us, it appears that production from the mine involved little or no user cost.

A somewhat later discussion of the effect of increasing return on price and profitability has already been referred to in the introduction to this study. It was there revealed that in the late 1920s F.R.E. Mauldon noted the tendency in Australia and the United States for discovery of richer coal mines to follow that of the poorer, resulting in an embarrassing surfeit of mined coal. Just a few years earlier, J.H. Clapham in his famous 'empty boxes' article also discussed the nature of return in the coal mining industry. Noting that in spite of the opening of new and highly efficient pits in Doncaster in Britain, the coal mining industry of that country might be experiencing a diminishing yield of coal 'per unit of resources', he suggested that in order to properly estimate the nature of return in the industry, it was necessary to consider events on the extensive margin abroad:

'That coal in Britain is being produced under conditions of diminishing returns is quite possible; but this is one of the cases in which we are least entitled to adopt a narrow national standpoint. One could hardly err in assuming that in Upper Silesia, or in the Transvaal, or in many parts of the United States the reverse is true; and as the world is fast becoming a single market for coal, and coal-mining a single world-industry like wheat-growing, any thorough inquiry would have not only to balance the virgin coal of Doncaster against the well-worked Lancashire field, but Britain against America or even against that wonderful coal-field through which, they say, the upper Yangtse-Kiang cuts its gorges. So far as our economist knows the work is not yet begun.'[4]

These empirical examples of the tendency to increasing return on the extensive margin were all discussed at a time when the influence of the first conservation movement was being felt and when the foundations were being laid for the essentially pessimistic neoclassical theory of the economics of exhaustible resources. These examples clearly supported Carey's idea that in some mineral industries, historical events would alter the ranking of resources to give increasing return on the extensive margin. Yet, in spite of the explicit acceptance of Carey's idea of increasing return on the extensive margin of agriculture, his case for similar treatment of mining was ignored.

Even in the recent past when conservationist sentiment has been high and when the essentially pessimistic literature based on Hotelling's 'seminal' article has experienced enormous growth, a number of empirically based examples of optimism about the availability of mineral resources have been offered. For example, in a recent discussion of contemporary and historical events in the Australian coal mining industry Gallagher and McColl concluded that:

'[C]oal resources and reserves both in Australia and in the world as a whole, are very large relative to current rates of extraction. This suggests that user cost or the inter-temporal opportunity cost is currently very small, perhaps negligible, relative to marginal extraction costs and that this situation is likely to persist.'[5]

In his comments on a paper delivered at the Resources Policy Conference in 1978, Marcus Digre gave an example which indicates that even when the long course of history is examined there may be observed a tendency for the rank order of mineral deposits to be altered as extension of the margin involves the exploitation of superior resources:

'In Norway, the mining industry started out about 400 years ago, first on small high-grade iron ore deposits and later on copper deposits. We have had at least 40-50 enterprises of some duration which have contributed very much in bringing Norway from a backward land close to the North Pole to a well developed welfare state.

I have looked into the ore deposits which these developments were founded on. If they had been left in the ground to this day, probably only two of them would even be considered for development, and Norway would have to be brought back to a neolithic stage before they would be utilized. Also here the technological factors decide. Exercises in mineral resource policies without thorough technological considerations may be misleading and dangerous.'[6]

Although there are other contemporary examples of the relevance of Carey's optimistic hypothesis of increasing return on the extensive margin which may be cited, it remains that in spite of the support for this idea from many of the authors whose work has been reviewed in this study and in spite of the eventual acceptance of Carey's hypothesis as it related to agriculture, the theoretical exhaustible resources literature produced during this century has been essentially pessimistic in its stance - emphasising that mining involves the 'cake eating' problem. It might be argued that this emphasis is appropriate for most mineral industries at most times. Even if this argument is correct, it is still the case that if some mineral industries are operating in an environment of increasing return on the extensive margin, it may be inappropriate to analyse them or to suggest policies for them on the basis of a theory which suggests that they are members of a broad class of industry in which present production involves user cost. A simple example will help clarify this point.

Ever since Gray and Hotelling noted that a monopolist is likely to retard output to a level below the competitively determined rate, it has been observed that the monopolist is the 'conservationist's friend'. Although the question of whether the monopolist will, in fact, retard output has been the subject of some contention in the recent literature, the idea that retardation of output by a monopolist will save valuable *in situ* mineral for future generations has been a pervasive one. Yet, if there is increasing return on the extensive margin it is possible that unmined mineral will become worthless; in which case welfare may be reduced:

'[T]he mere fact that monopoly is likely to result in greater conservation does not imply that it is socially optimal...remaining stocks of the mineral may, for instance, have no value at the end of the planning period and the effect of the monopoly could merely be to reduce welfare by its restrictive policies.'[7]

Recognition of the possibility of increasing return on the extensive margin allows a conclusion to be drawn about the significance of a monopolist's behaviour which, *cet. par.*, is very different from that suggested by a regime of decreasing return.[8] Nonetheless, each conclusion is drawn from the viewpoint of the neoclassical paradigm.

In spite of the evidence contained in the previously cited examples of increasing return on the extensive margin, the twentieth century development of the economic theory of exhaustible resources has generally involved emphasis on the idea that physical depletion of the contents of the mine involves a user cost. This being so, the question naturally arises as to why the pessimistic view has been triumphant.

Although there are possibly a number of factors which have contributed to this situation - not the least of which might be that this pessimism accurately reflects reality in most cases - there is a particular factor which warrants further consideration here. This factor relates to the influence of the perceived economic environment upon both the quantity and nature of contributions to the theoretical literature.

Discussing the waxing and waning of interest in political economy in England throughout the nineteenth century Walter Bagehot noted towards the end of the century that it was a subject in which greatest interest was shown during troubled times:

'Political Economy was, indeed, the favourite subject in England from about 1810 to 1840, and this to an extent which the present generation can scarcely comprehend. Indeed, old people are puzzled for an opposite reason; they can hardly understand the comparative disappearance of what was the principal topic in their youth. They mutter, with extreme surprise, "we hardly hear anything now about Political Economy; we used to hear of nothing so much". And the fundamental cause is the great improvement in the condition of the country. While the economic condition of countries is bad, men care for Political Economy, which may tell us how it is to be improved; when that condition is improved, Political Economy ceases to have the same popular interest, for it can no longer prescribe anything which helps the people's life.'[9]

If Bagehot's hypothesis is also relevant to natural resources so that the greatest interest in development of economic theories which deal with them is shown at times when fears are held for the capacity of the natural resource stock to maintain mankind's standard of living, then it is likely that an essentially pessimistic literature will evolve. Certainly, the literature which evolves is likely to be more pessimistic than one which experiences its greatest growth in times of little concern about the adequacy of the natural resource endowment. As was indicated in the introduction to this study, throughout this century the volume of contributions to the theoretical mineral economics literature has increased enormously at times of perceived natural resource crises.[10] If Bagehot's conclusions regarding political economy are also relevant in the case of natural resource economics then the last sentence in the quotation above may be rewritten as follows:

> While the natural resource outlook is bad, men care for
> natural resource economics, which may tell us how it is to be
> improved; when that condition is improved, natural resource
> economics ceases to have the same popular interest, for it
> can no longer prescribe anything which helps the people's
> life.

There appears to be a case for believing that the body of
neoclassical natural resource economics literature (including the
theoretical mineral economics literature) reflects the pessimism of
the times during which it has experienced its greatest growth.
Furthermore, in reflecting the pessimism of these times, this body
of literature may have a form which is sometimes sub-optimal
when it comes to the task of dealing with natural resource
economics in times of optimism. Just as a period of pessimism
about the natural resource endowment 'is never the best time to
examine long-term supply prospects because attention tends to
become so concentrated on the pressing issues that an objective
view of the longer term is hard to formulate',[11] so a period of
pessimism may not be the best time to make substantial additions
to the theoretical literature.[12]

Finally, does the triumph of the pessimistic view reflect only the
concern with the adequacy of natural resource stocks which was
prominent towards the end of the period reviewed here when a
definitive neoclassical treatment of the economics of exhaustible
resources was evolving, or is there some other relevant factor more
deeply rooted in the evolution of economic thought? In particular,
was the triumph of pessimism also the result of the supremacy of
Ricardo's abstract method over Adam Smith's and Carey's
integration of history with analysis? The majority of the contributions to the mineral economics literature which have been
reviewed in this study have constituted but a small part of larger
works devoted to economic principles in general. Although the
niggardliness of nature was naturally of concern to each of the
authors of these contributions, their works were clearly not
responses to a perceived natural resource crisis and, *regardless of
the methodological approach employed*, each of them at least
considered the relevance of both optimistic and pessimistic
scenarios. On the other hand, the contributions of Gray and
Hotelling which took the form of specific responses to the events
which were the concern of the first conservation movement
emphasised matters relating to those events and were generally

pessimistic in outlook. While it was the work of these authors which provided the foundation for the contemporary economic theory of exhaustible resources, the more dispassionate analyses of their peers and predecessors have been all but ignored.

Notes

1. The Duke's work was sufficiently influential to prompt a rebuttal from Alfred Marshall. A. Marshall, 'On rent', *Economic Journal*, vol. 3 (1893), reprinted in A. Marshall, *Principles of Economics*, 9th edn (Macmillan, London, 1961), editorial notes.

2. The Duke of Argyll, *The Unseen Foundations of Society* (John Murray, London, 1893).

3. Ibid., pp. 349-50. The Duke used the term 'machine' as a synonym for both mine and farm because he considered all three to be economically similar.

4. J.H. Clapham, 'Of empty economic boxes', *Economic Journal*, vol. 32 (1922), reprinted in the American Economic Association, *Readings in Price Theory* (George, Allen and Unwin, London, 1953).

5. D.R. Gallagher and G.D. McColl, 'Resource scarcity? Australian coal in a world perspective', paper presented at the 51st ANZAAS Congress, Brisbane, May, 1981, pp. 18-19.

6. M. Digre, Written contribution to Resources Policy Conference 78, *Resources Policy*, vol. 4, no. 3 (1978), p. 221.

7. K. Hartley and C. Tisdell, *Micro-Economic Policy* (John Wiley and Sons, Chichester, 1981), p. 329. Increasing return on the extensive margin is, of course, not the only factor which might cause unmined mineral to become worthless. Changes in other supply related factors and certain demand changes may also have the same effect. That this is so does not detract from the relevance of the argument in this quotation for cases where increasing return on the extensive margin is the relevant factor.

8. The nature of return on the extensive margin may also be particularly relevant to taxation policy. As I pointed out in my 1980 *Resources Policy* paper, a competitive firm operating in an environment of increasing return on the extensive margin is likely to earn quasi-rents early in its life which just compensate for losses incurred later on. To tax the quasi-rents as if they were true scarcity 'rents' could result in a significant misallocation of resources. T.J.C. Robinson, 'Classical foundations of the contemporary economic theory of non-renewable resources', *Resources Policy*, vol. 6, no. 4 (1980), p. 288.

9. W. Bagehot, *Economic Studies*, 2nd edn (Kelley, Clifton, 1973), pp. 201-2.

10. '[S]urprisingly it is only relatively recently that the study of [natural] resources has become established as a well-defined branch of economics - and even then it required a popular wave of concern over the long-run implications of a finite planet and the obvious degradation of our physical environment to alert economists in any number and persuade them to divert attention from their traditional fetishism with production, consumption and the pricing of consumed commodities.' J. McInerney, 'Natural resource economics: the basic analytical principles', in J.A. Butlin (ed.), *Economics and resources policy* (Longman, London, 1981), p. 32.

Conclusion

11. C. Robinson, 'The depletion of energy resources' in D.W. Pearce and J. Rose (eds), *The Economics of Natural Resource Depletion* (Macmillan, London, 1975), p. 21.

12. The desire to create a literature which deals with pressing problems of the time is, of course, quite rational. Difficulties arise, however, when that literature is based on premisses which are seen to be inappropriate from a more distant and detached viewpoint.

Bibliographical References

Adelman, M.A. (1976) 'The world oil cartel: scarcity, economics, and politics', *Quarterly Review of Economics and Business*, Summer Issue, pp. 7-18

Duke of Argyll (1893) *The Unseen Foundations of Society*, John Murray, London

American Economic Association (1953) *Readings in Price Theory*, George, Allen and Unwin, London

Arndt, H.W. (1978) *The Rise and Fall of Economic Growth*, Longman, Cheshire, Melbourne

Bagehot, W. (1973) *Economic Studies*, 2nd edn, Kelley, Clifton

Bambrick, S. (1979) *Australian Minerals and Energy Policy*, Australian National University Press, Canberra

Banks, F.E. (1976) *The Economics of Natural Resources*, Plenum Press, New York
_____ (1977) *Scarcity, Energy, and Economic Progress*, Lexington, Lexington
_____ (1983) *Resources and Energy*, Lexington, Lexington

Barnett, H.J. and Morse, C. (1963) *Scarcity and Growth*, Resources for the Future, Baltimore

Baumol, W.J. (1986) 'On the possibility of continuing expansion of finite resources', *Kyklos*, vol. 39, no. 2, pp. 167-79

Becker, G.S. (1976) *The Economic Approach to Human Behaviour*, University of Chicago Press, Chicago

Black, R.D.C. (ed.) (1981) *Papers and Correspondence of William Stanley Jevons*, Macmillan, London

Bladen, V.W. and Robson, J.M. (eds.) (1965) *Collected Works of John Stuart Mill*, vols 2 and 3, University of Toronto Press, Toronto

Blaug, M. (1958) *Ricardian Economics*, Greenwood Press, Westport, Connecticut
_____ (1968) *Economic Theory in Retrospect*, 2nd edn, Heinemann, London
_____ and Struges, P. (1983) *Who's Who in Economics*, Wheatsheaf, Brighton

Bohm-Bawerk, E.V. (1971) *The Positive Theory of Capital*, translated by W. Smart, Books for Libraries Press, New York

Bosson, R. and Varon, B. (1977) *The Mining Industry and the Developing Countries*, Oxford University Press, New York

Bottomore, T. (ed.) (1983) *A Dictionary of Marxist Thought*, Blackwell, Oxford

Boulding, K.E. (1966) *Economic Analysis*, 4th edn, Harper and Row, New York
_____ (1984) 'Sources of reasonable hope for the future', *American Economic Review*, Papers and Proceedings, vol. 74, no. 2, pp. 221-225

Breimeyer, H.F. (1978) 'Agriculture's three economies in a changing resource environment', *American Journal of Agricultural Economics*, vol. 60, no. 1, pp. 37-47

Bibliography

Brooks, D.B. (ed.) (1974) *Resource Economics: Selected Works of Orris C. Herfindahl*, Resources for the Future, Washington
_____ (1976) 'Conservation of minerals and of the environment', in Govett, G.J.S. and Govett, M.H. *World Minerals Supplies*, Elsevier, Amsterdam
Butlin, J.A. (ed.) (1981) *Economics and resources policy*, Longman, London
Cannan, E. (1917) *Theories of Production and Distribution*, London
_____ (1964) *A Review of Economic Theory*, Cass, London
Carey, H.C. (1963) *Principles of Social Science*, Kelley, New York
_____ (1967) *Principles of Political Economy*, Kelley, New York
_____ (1967) *The Past, the Present and the Future*, Kelley, New York
Carlisle, D. (1954) 'The economics of a fund resource with particular reference to mining', *American Economic Review*, vol. 44, no. 4, pp. 595-616
Casanova, P.G. (1981) *The Fallacy of Social Science Research*, Pergamon Press, New York
Cassel, G. (1923) *The Theory of Social Economy*, translated by J. McCabe, Fisher Unwin, London
_____ (1932) *The Theory of Social Economy*, translated by S.L. Barron, Harcourt Brace, New York
Chalmers, A.F. (1982) *What Is This Thing Called Science?*, 2nd edn, University of Queensland Press, St. Lucia
Ciriacy-Wantrup, S.V. (1952) *Resource Conservation Economics and Policies*, University of California Press, Berkley
Clapham, J.H. (1922) 'Of empty economic boxes', *Economic Journal*, vol. 32, reprinted in the American Economic Association (1953), *Readings in Price Theory*, George, Allen and Unwin, London
Clark, J.B. (1899) *The Distribution of Wealth*, Macmillan, New York
_____ (1907) *Essentials of Economic Theory*, Macmillan, New York
_____ (1910) 'The economics of waste and conservation', vol. 106, pp. 325-31
Cook, P.L. and Surrey, A.J. (1977) *Energy Policy*, Martin Robertson, London
Courtney, L.H. (1897) 'Jevons' coal question: thirty years after', *Royal Statistical Society Journal*, vol. 15, no. 4, pp. 789-810
Crabbe, P.J. (1983) 'The contribution of L.C. Gray to the economic theory of exhaustible natural resources and its roots in the history of economic thought', *Journal of Environmental Economics and Management*, vol. 10, pp. 195-220
_____ (1986) 'Gray and Hotelling: a reply', *Journal of Environmental Economics and Management*, vol. 13, no. 3, pp. 295-300
Critchley, M. (1979) *The Divine Banquet of the Brain and Other Essays*, Raven Press, New York
Cropsey, J. (1955) 'What is Welfare Economics', *Ethics*, vol. 65, no. 2, pp. 116-25
Dale, L.L. (1984) 'The pace of mineral depletion in the United States', *Land Economics*, vol. 60, no. 3, pp. 255-267
Dasgupta, P.S. and Heal, G. (1979) *Economic Theory and Exhaustible Resources*, James Nisbet and Co., Welwyn
_____ Gilbert, R. and Stiglitz, J. (1982) *Strategic considerations in invention and innovation: the case of natural resources*, International Centre for Economics and Related Disciplines, London
Davidson, P. (1979) 'The economics of natural resources', *Challenge*, vol. 22, pp. 40-46
Devarajan, S. and Fisher, A.C. (1981) 'Hotelling's "Economics of Exhaustible Resources", fifty years later', *Journal of Economic Literature*, vol. 19, pp. 65-73
Dictionary of National Biography, 1931-40, Oxford University Press, Oxford

Bibliography

Digre, M. I. (1978) Written contribution to Resources Policy Conference 78, *Resources Policy*, vol. 4, no. 3, p. 221

Ely, R.T., Hess, R.H. and Carver, T.N. (1971) *National Prosperity*, Johnson Reprint, New York

Farrow, S. (1985) 'Testing the efficiency of extraction from a stock resource', *Journal of Political Economy*, vol. 93, no. 2, pp. 452-487

Fay, C.R. (1929) *Great Britain from Adam Smith to the Present Day*, Longmans, Green, London

Fine, B. (1982) 'Landed property and the distinction between royalty and rent', *Land Economics*, vol. 58, no. 3, pp. 338-350

Fisher, A.C. (1981) *Resource and environmental economics*, Cambridge University Press, Cambridge

Fisher, I. (1970) *The Theory of Interest*, Kelley, New York

_____ (1982) *The Rate of Interest*, Garland, New York

Fitzgibbons, A. and Cochrane, S. (1978) 'Optimal rate of natural resource depletion', *Resources Policy*, vol. 4, no. 3, pp. 166-171

Flux, A.W. (1904) *Economic Principles*, Methuen, London

Fraser, L.M. (1947) *Economic Thought and Language*, A and C Black, London

Friedman, M. and R. (1980) *Free to Choose*, Harcourt Brace Jovanovich, New York

Gaffney, M. (ed.) (1967) *Extractive Resources and Taxation*, University of Wisconsin Press, Madison

Gallagher, D.R. and McColl, G.D. (1981) 'Resource scarcity? Australian coal in a world perspective', paper presented at the 51st ANZAAS Congress, Brisbane

Georgescu-Roegen, N. (1971) *The Entropy Law and the Economic Process*, Harvard University Press, Cambridge

Gordon, H.S. (1952) 'On a misinterpretation of the law of diminishing returns in Marshall's *Principles*', *Canadian Journal of Economics*, vol. 18, reprinted in J.E. Wood (ed.) (1982) *Alfred Marshall: Critical Assessments*, vol. III, Croom Helm, London

Govett, G.J.S. and Govett, M.H. (1976) *World Mineral Supplies*, Elsevier, Amsterdam

Gowdy, J.M. (1984) 'Marx and resource scarcity: an institutionalist approach', *Journal of Economic Issues*, vol. 18, no. 2, pp. 393-400

Graham, W.S. (1980) 'The selective interpretation of Adam Smith', *Journal of Economic Issues*, March, pp. 119-142

Gray, A. (1931) *The Development of Economic Doctrine*, Longmans, Green

Gray, L.C. (1913) 'The economic possibilities of conservation', *Quarterly Journal of Economics*, vol. 27, pp. 497-519

_____ (1914) 'Rent under the assumption of exhaustibility', *Quarterly Journal of Economics*, vol. 28, reprinted in Gaffney, M. (ed.) (1967) *Extractive Resources and Taxation*, University of Wisconsin Press, Madison

Groenewegen, P.D. (1982) 'History and political economy: Smith, Marx and Marshall', *Australian Economic Papers*, vol. 21, no. 38, pp. 1-17

Gruen, F.H. (ed.) (1983) *Surveys of Australian Economics*, vol. III, George Allen and Unwin, Sydney

_____ and Hillman, A.L. (1980) 'Economic issues pertinent to energy policy: a schematic review of market and non-market perspectives', ANU Centre for Economic Policy Research, Discussion Paper no. 14

Halvorsen, R. and Smith, T.F. (1984) 'On measuring natural resource scarcity', *Journal of Political Economy*, vol. 92, no. 5, pp. 954-964

Hartley, K. and Tisdell, C. (1981) *Micro-Economic Policy*, John Wiley and Sons, Chichester

Hawtrey, R.G. (1926) *The Economic Problem*, Longmans, Green, London

Hendrikx, H.P. (1982) 'The improvement hypothesis: a study of the global trade in non-renewable resources', unpublished M. Econ. thesis, University of Queensland

Herfindahl, O.C. (1955) 'Some fundamentals of mineral economics', *Land Economics*, vol. 31, pp. 131-38

_____ (1967) 'Depletion and economic theory' in Gaffney, M. (ed.), *Extractive Resources and Taxation*, University of Wisconsin Press, Madison

_____ and Kneese, A.V. (1974) *Economic Theory of Natural Resources*, Merrill, Columbus

Hicks, J.R. (1946) *Value and Capital*, 2nd edn, Oxford University Press, Oxford

Hillman, A.L. and Long, N.V. (1982) 'Substitutes for a depletable resource and the monopolistic conservationist presumption', *Australian Economic Papers*, vol. 21, no. 38, pp. 193-99

Hollander, S. (1973) *The Economics of Adam Smith*, Heinemann, London

Hoskold, H.D. (1903) 'The valuation of mines of definite average income', *American Institute of Mining Engineers Transactions*, vol. 33, reprinted in VanLandingham, S.L. (1983) *Economic Evaluation of Mineral Property*, Hutchinson Ross, Stroudsburg, Penn.

Hotelling, H. (1931) 'The economics of exhaustible resources', *Journal of Political Economy*, vol. 39, no. 2, pp. 137-75

Howard, M.C. and King, J.E. (1975) *The Political Economy of Marx*, Longman, Burnt Mill

Hutchison, T.W. (1965) *The Significance and Basic Postulates of Economic Theory*, Kelley, New York

_____ (1978) *On Revolutions and Progress in Economic Knowledge*, Cambridge University Press, Cambridge

Hyman, E.L. (1984) 'Natural resource economics: relevance in planning and management', *Resources Policy*, vol. 10, no. 3, pp. 163-176

Ise, J. (1925) 'The theory of value as applied to natural resources', *American Economic Review*, vol. 15, pp. 284-91

_____ (1926) *The United States Oil Policy*, Yale University Press, New Haven

Jackman, W.T. (1962) *The Development of Transportation in Modern England*, Cass, London

Jevons, W.S. (1877) *The Principles of Science*, 2nd edn, Macmillan, London

_____ (1906) *The Coal Question*, 3rd edn, Macmillan, London

Kapp, K.W. (1971) *The Social Costs of Private Enterprise*, 2nd edn, Schocken Books, New York

Kay, J.A. and Mirrlees, J.A. (1975) 'The desirability of natural resource depletion', in Pearce, D.W. and Rose, J. (eds), *The Economics of Natural Resource Depletion*, Macmillan, London

Kenwood, A.G. and Lougheed, A.L. (1982) *Technological Diffusion and Industralisation before 1914*, Croom Helm, London

Keynes, J.M. (1936) *The General Theory of Employment Interest and Money*, Macmillan, London

Keynes, J.N. (1904) *The Scope and Method of Political Economy*, 2nd edn, Macmillan, London

King, W.I. (1916) 'Does conservation involve cost?' *Quarterly Journal of Economics*, vol. 30, pp. 595-600

Knight, F.H. (1933) *Risk Uncertainty and Profit*, London School of Economics and Political Science, Reprints of Scarce Tracts in Economic and Political Science

Lazarsfeld, P.F., Pasanella, A.K. and Rosenberg, M. (eds) (1972) *Continuities in the Language of Social Research*, Free Press, New York

Levhari, D. and Liviatan, N. (1977) 'Notes on Hotelling's economics of exhaustible resources', *Canadian Journal of Economics*, vol. 10, no. 2, pp. 177-92

Lewis, B. (1972) *Coal Mining in the Eighteenth and Nineteenth Centuries*, Longman, London

Little, I.M.D. (1953) *The Price of Fuel*, Oxford University Press, London

Lloyd, P.J. (ed.) (1984) *Mineral Economics in Australia*, George, Allen and Unwin, Sydney

Lougheed, A.L. (1985) 'The cyanide process and gold extraction in Australasia, 1888-1913', University of Queensland, Department of Economics, Working Papers in Economics, No. 51

Lutz, F. and V. (1951) *The Theory of Investment of the Firm*, Princeton University Press, Princeton

McAllister, A.L. (1976) 'Price technology and ore reserves', in Govett, G.J.S. and Govett, M.H.(eds), *World Mineral Supplies*, Elsevier, Amsterdam

McInerney, J. (1981) 'Natural resource economics: the basic analytical principles' in Butlin, J.A. (ed.), *Economics and Resources Policy*, Longman, London

Malthus, T.R. (1963) *Definitions in Political Economy*, Kelley, New York

Marschak, J. (1965) 'Economics of language', *Behavioural Science*, vol. 10, no. 2, pp. 135-40

Marsh, G.P. (1965) *Man and Nature*, Belknap Press of Harvard University Press, Cambridge

Marshall, A. (1885) *The Economics of Industry*, 3rd edn, Macmillan, London
_____ (1893) 'On rent', *Economic Journal*, vol. 3, reprinted in Marshall, A. (1961) *Principles of Economics*, 9th edn, Macmillan, London, editorial notes
_____ (1920) *Principles of Economics*, 8th edn, 1949 resetting, Macmillan, London
_____ (1927) *Industry and Trade*, Macmillan, London
_____ (1961) *Principles of Economics*, 9th (variorum) edn, Macmillan, London

Marx, K. (1951) *Theories of Surplus Value*, Bonner, G.A. and Burns, E. translators, Lawrence and Wishart, London
_____ (1954) *Capital*, Progress Press, Moscow
_____ (1969) *Theories of Surplus Value*, part II, Lawrence and Wishart, London

Mauldon, F.R.E. (1929) *The Economics of Australian Coal*, Melbourne University Press, Melbourne

Medawar, P. (1982) *Pluto's Republic*, Oxford University Press, Oxford

Mill, J.S. (1895) *Principles of Political Economy*, Routledge, London

Mitchell, B.R. (1984) *Economic Development of the British Coal Industry 1800-1914*, Cambridge University Press, Cambridge

Morrow, G.R. (1973) *The Ethical and Economic Theories of Adam Smith*, Kelley, Clifton

Neale, W.C. (1982) 'Language and economics', *Journal of Economic Issues*, vol. 16, no. 2, pp. 355-69

Nef, J.U. (1966) *The Rise of the British Coal Industry*, Cass, London

Newcomb, S. (1886) *Principles of Political Economy*, Harper and Bros, New York

Ohle, E.L. (1972) 'Evaluation of iron ore deposits', *Economic Geology*, vol. 67, reprinted in VanLandingham, S.L. (ed.) (1983) *Economic Evaluation of Mineral Property*, Hutchinson Ross, Stroudsburg, Penn.

Orchard, J.E. (1922) 'The rent of mineral lands', *Quarterly Journal of Economics*, vol. 36, pp. 290-318

Oser, J. (1970) *The Evolution of Economic Thought*, 2nd edn, Harcourt, Brace and World

Palgrave, R.H.I. (ed.) (1910) *Dictionary of Political Economy*, Macmillan, London

Pantaleoni, M. (1898) *Pure Economics*, Macmillan, London

Passmore, J. (1974) *Man's Responsibility for Nature*, Duckworth, London

Bibliography

Pearce, D.W. (1976) *Environmental Economics*, Longman, London
_____ and Rose, J. (eds) (1975) *The Economics of Natural Resource Depletion*, Macmillan, London
Penrose, E.T. (1968) *The Theory of the Growth of the Firm*, Blackwell, Oxford
Perelman, M. (1974) 'An application of Marxian theory to environmental economics', *Review of Radical Political Economics*, Fall
Peterson, R.M. and Fisher, A.C. (1977) 'The exploitation of extractive resources a survey', *Economic Journal*, vol. 87, pp. 681-721
Pindyck, R.S. (1978) 'The optimal exploration and produciton of non-renewable resources', *Journal of Political Economy*, vol. 86, no. 51, pp. 841-61
Price-Williams, R. (1889) 'The coal question', *Journal of the Royal Statistical Society*, vol. 52, pp. 1-55
Raggatt, H.G. (1968) *Mountains of Ore*, Landsdowne, Melbourne
Ray, G.F. (1979) 'Energy economics - a random walk in history', *Energy economics*, vol. 1, no. 3, pp. 139-43
_____ (1984) 'Mineral reserves: projected lifetimes and security of supply', *Resources Policy*, vol. 10, no. 2, pp. 75-80
_____ and Uhlman, L. (1979) *The Innovation Process in the Energy Industries*, Cambridge University Press, Cambridge
Ricardo, D. (1911) *The Principles of Political Economy and Taxation*, Dent, London
Robinson, C. (1974) *The Energy 'Crisis' and British Coal*, Hobart Paper no. 59, Institute of Economic Affairs, London
_____ (1975) 'The depletion of energy resources', in Pearce, D.W. and Rose, J. (eds) *The Economics of Natural Resource Depletion*, Macmillan, London
Robinson, J. (1950) *The Economics of Imperfect Competition*, Macmillan, London
Robinson, T.J.C. (1977) 'The costs of ocean transport of bulk minerals', *International Journal of Transport Economics*, vol. 4, no. 4, pp. 317-29
_____ (1979) 'The distinction between coking coal and steaming coal: implications for the assessment of energy resources', *Energy Policy*, vol. 7, no. 1, pp. 69-71
_____ (1979) 'An assessment of the classical economists' contribution to the economics of non-renewable resources', paper presented to the Eighth Conference of Economists, Melbourne
_____ (1980) 'Classical foundations of the contemporary economic theory of non-renewable resources', *Resources Policy*, vol. 6, no. 4, pp. 278-89
_____ (1981) 'The economics of classificatory systems and its relevance for the classification of natural resources', paper presented to the fifty-first ANZAAS Conference, Brisbane
_____ (1981) 'Postscript, Classical foundations of the contemporary economic theory of non-renewable resources' *Resources Policy*, vol. 7, no. 4, p. 289
_____ (1986) 'The nature of physical return in mining', Queensland Institute of Technology, Working Papers in Management, no. 3
St. Clair, O. (1965) *Key to Ricardo*, Kelley, New York
Schumpeter, J.A. (1954) *History of Economic Analysis*, George, Allen and Unwin, London
_____ (1976) *Capitalism, Socialism and Democracy*, 5th edn, George, Allen and Unwin, London
Scott, A.D. (1953) 'Notes on user cost', *Economic Journal*, vol. 63, pp. 368-384
Scott, A.T. (1967) 'The theory of the mine under conditions of certainty', in Gaffney, M. (ed.), *Extractive Resources and Taxation*, University of Wisconsin Press, Madison
Simon, J.L. (1981) *The Ultimate Resource*, Martin Robertson, Oxford

Bibliography

Smith, A. (1869) *An Enquiry into the Nature and Causes of the Wealth of Nations*, Rogers, J.E.T. (ed.), Oxford University Press, Oxford

___ (1904) *An Enquiry into the Nature and Causes of the Wealth of Nations*, Methuen, London

___ (1970) *An Enquiry into the Nature and Causes of the Wealth of Nations*, Skinner, A. (ed.), Penguin, Harmondsworth

___ (1976) *An Enquiry into the Nature and Causes of the Wealth of Nations*, Campbell, R.H. Skinner, A.S. and Todd, W.B. (eds), Clarendon, Oxford

Smith, G.A. (1982) 'Natural resource economic theory of the first conservation movement (1895-1927)', *History of Political Economy*, vol. 14, no. 4, pp. 483-495

___ (1986) 'Gray and Hotelling: a comment', *Journal of Environment Economics and Management*, vol 13, no. 3, pp. 292-294

Smith, V.K. (ed.) (1979) *Scarcity and Growth Reconsidered*, Resources for the Future, Washington

Soddy, F. (1922) *Cartesian Economics*, Hendersons, London

Solow, R.M. (1974) 'The economics of resources or the resources of economics', *American Economic Review*, vol. 64, pp. 1-14

Sorley, W.R. (1889) 'Mining royalties and their effect on the iron and coal trades', *Royal Statistical Society Journal*, vol. 52, pp. 60-98

Soule, G. (1955) *Ideas of the Great Economists*, Mentor, New York

Steele, H. (1967) 'Natural resource taxation: resource allocation and distribution implications' in Gaffney, M (ed.), *Extractive Resources and Taxation*, University of Wisconsin Press, Madison

Sraffa, P. (ed.) (1951-1973) *The Works and Correspondence of David Ricardo*, 11 vols, Cambridge University Press, London

Stigler, G. (1946) *Production and Distribution Theories*, Macmillan, New York

___ (1950) *The Theory of Price*, Macmillan, New York

___ (1985) 'The economies of scale', *Journal of Law and Economics*, vol. 1, no. 1, pp. 54-71

___ (1966) *The Theory of Price*, 3rd edn, Macmillan, New York

Subbarayudu, C. (1977) 'Ricardo's definition of rent', *Indian Economic Journal*, vol. 25, no. 1

Taussig, F.W. (1923) *Principles of Economics*, 3rd edn, Macmillan, New York

Tisdell, C.A. (1982) *Microeconomics of Markets*, John Wiley and Sons, Brisbane

Turner, J.F. (1912), 'Henry C. Carey's attitude toward the Ricardian theory of rent', *Quarterly Journal of Economics*, vol. 26, pp. 644-72, reprinted in J.C. Wood (ed.) (1985) *David Ricardo Critical Assessments*, vol. III, Croom Helm, London

Turvey, R. (1955) 'A Finnish contribution to rent theory', *Economic Journal*, vol. 65, pp. 346-48

Ulph, A.M. (1978) 'A model of resource depletion with multiple grades', *Economic Record*, vol. 54, pp. 334-45

VanLandingham, S.L. (ed.) (1983) *Economic Evaluation of Mineral Property*, Hutchinson Ross, Stroudsburg, Penn.

Wahl, S. (1983) *Investment Appraisal and Economic Evaluation of Mining Enterprise*, Trans Tech, Clausthal-Zellerfeld

Walker, F.A. (1887) *Political Economy*, 3rd edn, Macmillan, London

Weinstein, M.C. and Zeckhauser, R.J. (1974) 'Use patterns for depletable and recyclable resources', *Symposium on the Economics of Exhaustible Resources*, Review of Economic Studies, pp. 67-88

Wiles, P.J.D. (1956) *Price Cost and Output*, Blackwell, Oxford

Bibliography

Wood, J.C. (ed.) (1982) *Alfred Marshall: Critical Assessments*, Croom Helm, London

Wood, J.C. (ed.) (1985) *David Ricardo Critical Assessments*, vol. III, Croom Helm, London

Young, A.A. (1928) 'Increasing returns and economic progress', *Economic Journal*, vol. 38, pp. 527-42

Zannetos, Z.S. (1966) *The Theory of Oil Tankship Rates*, M.I.T. Press, Cambridge

Index

191

DATE DUE

AUG 07 2004